Early Praise for
In Search of the Owl

I'll always remember tall slender Levi on fieldtrips keenly observing things in nature with his camera always at the ready. He took in all of the outdoors, animals, birds, plants and terrain. He passed these traits on to his children. In writing this tribute to her father, Dr. Jean Mohler Sidinger displays her own love of the outdoors. When she describes a scene she and her father visited many years ago you are there with them. You hear the breeze push gently through the tall grass. You see the ripples on an otherwise placid pond. You smell the fragrant flowers along the path. And you hear the flock of redwings settling in the cattails. Dr. Sidinger's descriptive words flow like poetry through this entire memoir.

— **Alfred G. Larson, Honorary Board Member**
Golden Eagle Chapter
National Audubon Society

That Jean Mohler Sidinger inherited her father's eye for the small but incredibly complex workings of the natural world is evident in her writing. Her descriptions of the Great Plains landscape are like the landscape itself—seemingly sparse, but filled with life and understanding.

I knew Jean's father, Levi, only in his later years. We shared many interests even though in ages we were several decades apart. In the 1940s and early-1950s, Levi was a biologist for the Nebraska Game and Parks Commission—a field biologist, a man who learned not only from books but by spending days and years in grasslands and along shallow prairie rivers. His curiosity and love for nature never diminished through his long life. He wrote prolifically of his discoveries and observations, in scientific publications and in the popular press to tutor those sharing his interests but not his experience. For most of his life he was a teacher.

Jean's writing captures that man, not in maudlin sentimentality, but with words telling of her love for her father, and her father's love of the natural world. The book is the story of her quest to accept his death, her search for understanding, her search for the wisdom of the owl. It is a journey through nature, to some of the places she had been with her father; but it is also a journey through time, through her father's past and her times with him. It is a search to understand, to come to terms with the loss of a loved one, of life and death. She searched for the answers where her father had searched—in the natural world. Jean found the wisdom of the owl. Her writing of the search is at once poignant and yet with the keen eye of a field biologist, the way her father had seen life. It is a loving tribute to a unique man.

—Jon Farrar, Former Senior Editor,
NEBRASKAland Magazine

The death of a parent, no matter how old they are, can leave a huge hole within our hearts. The dying of our parent can also spring us into the experience of orphanhood and ask us to weave the golden thread of love as we retell a story of loving.

In this powerful book Jean Mohler Sidinger masterfully captures her father's love of nature and her endearing love of her father as she tells the story of his death and of his life.

Telling the story assists us in our grieving to a place of restoring, in order to reinvest our energy of honor and memory. You will be carried on the silence of the owl wings as you read this subtle masterpiece, which is profoundly unscripted. Let it inspire you to weave the tattered threads of grief into the golden threads of loving memory.

—Patty Luckenbach, D.D.
Associate Minister, Mile Hi Church-Science of Mind and Spirit, Lakewood, CO
Author of *The Kingdom of Heart*, and *The Land of Tears is a Secret Place*

In Search of the Owl

A father's death
begins a quest for
a deeper understanding
...of life.

A Memoir

JEAN E. SIDINGER

In Search of the Owl:
A father's death begins a quest for
a deeper understanding…of life.

Copyright © 2021 by Jean E. Sidinger

All rights reserved. No part of this publication may be reproduced, distributed, or transmitted in any form or by any means, without prior written permission from the publisher.

Published by:

SS

SILVER • SAGE
Denver, Colorado
www.jeansidinger.com

Illustrations (Graphite and Ink Drawings) © 2020
by Jean E. Sidinger

Cover & Interior Book Layout
by Veronica Yager, YellowStudios

Paperback ISBN: 978-1-7357045-0-0
Library of Congress Control Number: 2020922038

Publisher's Note: The events and conversations in this book have been set down to the best of the author's ability, although some names and details have been changed to protect the privacy of individuals.

*To the
memory of
my beloved father,
Levi L. Mohler*

CONTENTS

PROLOGUE
A Few Days in February
i

PART ONE
Time of Death: Spring
1

PART TWO
A Surreal Summer
119

PART THREE
Finally, Fall
159

PART FOUR
Winter Awakenings
209

PART FIVE
The Second Spring
247

ACKNOWLEDGMENTS
271

ABOUT THE AUTHOR
273

PROLOGUE

A Few Days in February

February 13

Knock, knock, knock. I stood in front of my dad's door at the retirement center, the balloon I held behind my back bobbing above my shoulder. I'd driven two days and slept in a local motel the night before so I could be there. My father opened the door, smiling from ear to ear.

"Good morning, Jean."

"Happy birthday!" I leaned in and gave him a big hug. We stepped into his tidy apartment and I added my gift to a stack of presents waiting to be opened.

He and I had eaten dinner together the night before. We had caught up and made plans for his birthday.

"Are you ready for breakfast?" he asked.

"Sure, let's go."

"I think I'll take my balloon with me."

"Let me tie it to one of your belt loops so your hands will be free."

The red, yellow, and blue Mylar balloon danced after him down the hallway as we headed for breakfast. As always, his thick silver hair was neatly groomed. One of his favorite string ties was threaded through his shirt collar; the presence of the bolo tie indicated today was a special day. It certainly was. My dad was turning ninety-four.

After our trip through the buffet line, I photographed him at the table with his one strip of bacon, slice of whole wheat toast, oatmeal topped with raisins and brown sugar, orange juice, one-third of a banana, and cup of hot water. This was a typical breakfast for him, although he varied his selections from day to day. One thing that made him easy to be around was he wasn't rigid in his behavior, including eating habits, as often happens with someone advanced in years.

Mom had died three years earlier, so my dad was especially glad when one of his children came to visit. He knew we would get him out and about and he loved that. Before we left the table, we reviewed the activities and outings we had discussed the evening before.

After breakfast he opened his cards and gifts, including those from my sister, Lois, and my brother, Robert. The present from me was small, but I had deemed it perfect. It was a spiral-bound book, *Birder's Life List and Diary*, a journal formatted for him to record information about birds he had seen throughout his life. These days the birds he watched were at the birdbath or in the stately ponderosa just beyond his window. When he opened my gift, he smiled broadly and proceeded to thumb through the pages.

"This is exactly what I need. Thank you, Jean."

"You've written about birds and you must have pages and pages of observations from those Audubon outings. And you've told me your diaries are full of notes about birds."

He laughed. "Yes, and I've stuck in countless little slips of paper with information I wanted to remember about that day's birds."

"And you had all those years in the field with your wildlife work. I hope this will help you consolidate information about the birds you've observed."

"Indeed. It really will be helpful. I can't wait to get started on it."

"How many species have you seen?"

"I don't know for sure, but several hundred." He held up the book and added, "Now I'll be able to find out."

Just before ten thirty that morning, we headed upstairs for a Valentine's Day party. Yes, it was February thirteenth, but holidays were often celebrated a day early at Hillcrest Retirement Center because many residents opted to spend holidays with their families away from the facility.

"Happy birthday, Levi," someone called out from across the room as we arrived. Daddy nodded in thanks and someone else stuck out a hand in congratulations. I smiled from the sidelines.

Three rows of folding chairs had been arranged facing an upright piano in the large multi-purpose room. Some were moved aside as folks in wheelchairs arrived. A middle-aged staff member whom I hadn't met welcomed everyone, made a few announcements, and settled herself onto the piano bench while a handful of residents assembled at the front of the room: eight individuals, including my dad. He stood tall and proud, towering above the other members of the group. They had dubbed themselves the Over-the-Hill Crest Singers. Though few in number, their enthusiasm coupled with the piano accompaniment produced enjoyable entertainment. I listened with pride to my dad's strong yet gentle voice, singing in harmony with the higher ranges of the female vocalists. Their repertoire included old favorites such as "I'll Be Loving You Always." Listening to the lazy pace of the reassuring lyrics, I *did* feel loved. During their rendition of "Let Me Call You Sweetheart," several people in the small audience were singing along, swaying side to side in their seats.

Everyone watched as Hillcrest's director crowned the beaming King and Queen of Hearts, chosen by a vote of the residents. I was there two years ago when that tradition began and Daddy was crowned the first King of Hearts. He was surprised, but I wasn't. An unwritten rule immediately took hold that no one could be elected a second time.

I had ordered a sheet cake from the local Albertsons for Daddy's birthday. It was frosted in white, decorated with a profusion of colors, and edged with a thick piping of yellow. HAPPY BIRTHDAY LEVI 94 was written on a light blue frosting banner. The staff had placed the cake on the table with the other goodies.

After the singing and announcement of the king and queen, folks ambled over to the refreshment table. It was covered with a thin plastic cloth strewn with red hearts. Offerings included fresh strawberries, candy, and valentine sugar cookies. Almost everyone wanted a slice of cake and a glass of red punch. So the Valentine's party turned into a birthday party as well. Scattered throughout the upstairs loft, the almost thirty attendees clustered in small groups, some sitting and others standing, celebrating with lively conversation and laughter. In that group, birthdays are a highly valued commodity; my father was one of the oldest and most mobile residents. Individuals who were blessed to be living so independently well into their nineties were inspirational role models.

Early that evening, Daddy and I dressed up, he in his best suit, I in my little black dress. I had made reservations for six o'clock dinner at Emilio's, the upscale restaurant in the downtown luxury Grove Hotel. When I called, I had mentioned it was my father's birthday, so the *maître d'*, as well as our waitress, fussed over him appropriately. Their eyes grew big and they broke into smiles when they learned his age. "You're ninety-four? You don't look a day over eighty," the waitress said, shaking his hand.

After we finished our meal, they surprised us with a slice of strawberry cheesecake topped with a lighted candle. After making a wish, he blew out the candle. Even given all the eating we'd done that day, we didn't hesitate to consume the yummy dessert.

We were in no hurry to leave. Our arc-shaped booth with its high cushioned back was comfortable. During a lull in our conversation, I decided it was a good time to revisit a topic from awhile back. I placed my hands on the edge of the table.

"Are you still planning to be in touch with me after you die?"

"Yes. I will be in touch," he said, closing his eyes briefly, a peaceful look coming over his face.

"I'm so glad." I reached over and took his large, wrinkled hand. "Thank you."

February 14

For Valentine's Day, we'd been invited by two of Daddy and Mother's longtime friends to have lunch at their secluded cabin in the mountains. My dad had stopped driving a few years earlier, so he was thoroughly enjoying the rare opportunity to be away from the city. Clear blue skies made our hour-long drive particularly enjoyable.

I had heard much about Al and Hilda but had never met them. Their cabin was indeed that: small and rustic, nestled into the forest but facing a large grassy opening to the north. Mother and Daddy had become acquainted with them through the Audubon Society. The two couples shared a love of nature, especially bird-watching.

They saw us parking and met us with the door—and their arms—wide open.

"Welcome, welcome, Jean. We've heard so much about you. And happy belated birthday, Levi."

"Thanks for having us up today," I answered.

"Of course. Glad you could bring your dad to see us. We don't get together much now that we're all *old folks*." They all laughed.

With the cozy warmth of the cook stove and their genuineness, I immediately felt at home. I turned to Hilda and said, "So, this huge window must be where you make those observations you write about in the Audubon newsletter."

"That's right. That's why I call the column 'Out the Kitchen Window.'"

We sat at the checkered oilcloth-covered, round table positioned near the window. Lunch was ready. What had smelled so enticing when we walked in turned out to be hearty homemade vegetable-beef soup. As we ate our soup and sandwiches, the easy flow of conversation continued while we watched Oregon juncos and black-capped chickadees at the bird feeders.

Always on the lookout for signs of wildlife, Daddy had spotted turkey tracks in the mud beside the car when we arrived. But it was more than an hour into our visit before the large birds appeared. Four tom turkeys made themselves at home grazing on the bare patch of winter lawn. We spent much of our remaining time there watching and photographing the notoriously elusive birds. Before we were ready to depart the turkeys climbed single file up a steep, ponderosa-covered slope and disappeared.

When we left, we retraced our route back to the main highway. After a few miles, we stopped to explore the nearby town of Idaho City. We browsed for several minutes inside Donna's Place, a shop overflowing with kitschy magnets and Idaho mugs. I asked my dad, "Are you going to buy something?"

He answered, "I don't see anything I need." I smiled to myself, thinking of all the places that would go out of business if people exercised self-control and only purchased something when they needed it. But he did buy something: a small, turquoise-colored tumbled stone. A gift for me.

"This is a lovely keepsake, Daddy. Thank you. It will remind me of today."

February 15

Our fourth and final day together flew by. Our plans had included a stroll in my dad's favorite park. A full schedule of activities brought us to late afternoon, without our walk. We had been excited about the outing, and I had a sinking feeling when I realized it might not happen. There wasn't enough time to go before dinner.

"You know, Daddy, if we eat as soon as the dining room opens, we can go to the park afterward. It might be getting dark, but I think it could work."

His face lit up. "Great. Let's do that."

When we arrived, daylight was indeed fading and there was a damp chill in the air. We walked slowly side by side along the wide sidewalk, our eyes adjusting to the waning light. We could barely discern a flock of Canada geese feeding on the broad expanse of park lawn a couple of hundred feet ahead. Our goal was to reach Dad's favorite rock bench. Once there, he suggested we sit for a few minutes. I took the heavy, fringed muffler from around my neck and folded it to create a cushion for him against the cold granite. We sat close together and I slipped my coated arm in through his. I could feel his warmth. We listened to the evening, to the frequent calls of the wild geese and ducks either flying in to join others of their kind in the grazing flock or departing for elsewhere. Several times a pair of waterfowl flew so close we could hear their strong wing strokes. The sky to the west radiated a pocket of silver light, silhouetting the skeleton trees of winter.

As we readied to leave, we turned back toward the east. An almost-full moon had cleared the horizon and was showing itself through the mist. Daddy gathered his cane; I collected my scarf and wrapped it around the upturned collar of his coat so his ears were almost covered. Although it was dark, the rising moon illumined the pathway ahead. Nonetheless, we picked our way carefully. Scarcely talking, savoring the night sounds and the brisk air, we walked slowly, arm-in-arm as two sweethearts might have done.

Back at Hillcrest we hugged and reluctantly said our goodbyes. It was difficult to leave him, especially considering the uncertainty as to when we would be together again. As I drove away I saw my dear father standing at the window near the entry, waving. I waved back. Still feeling the intensity of the loving connection we had shared on our quiet stroll at dusk, I became aware of the desperation in my throat and the tears filling my eyes.

PART ONE

Time of Death: Spring

Before the Owl

Long before that walk in the park, long before thoughts of my father's death were on anyone's mind, a unique series of events had taken place. Had they not, the *in search of the owl* metaphor that was to become both intriguing and pleasing to me never would have come to be.

I must share the story with you.

It began many years ago, perhaps in 1909, the year my father was born, or perhaps years or even eons earlier when life itself began. Growing up on a homestead on the Nebraska plains, its windswept land devoid of trees, my father became intimately acquainted with the natural world that surrounded him. Young Levi was fascinated when one summer morning his mother showed him her discovery. While tending her garden beside their sod house, she had spied a tiny bird's nest in the crotch of an upright bean plant. Within it nestled a few even tinier eggs.

The conversation may have gone like this, with her telling my father, less than five years old, "You must not touch the nest or the eggs."

"Why?"

"Because they are a promise of new life. Just like some of our chicken eggs hatch and become baby chicks, baby birds are growing inside these eggs."

"They must be little."

"Yes, they are. But if we don't bother the nest, the mother will sit on the eggs many hours each day until her babies hatch. We don't want to scare her away."

"I want to see the baby birds when they come out."

"I do too."

"How long will it be?"

"Several days. We will watch for them together."

That was among the earliest of my father's recollections of the wonders of nature. His love for the natural order enriched his life even to his final day, when my brother, Robert, in the last telephone conversation with his father, assured him the migrating sandhill cranes were filling the Nebraska skies that morning. I was told Daddy responded weakly, "That's good," as if to say, "And all is right with the world."

First Sunday of Spring

My dad had been on my mind all day, so that evening, I dialed his Boise number. As the phone rang I anticipated another lively conversation. When he answered, I was alarmed to hear his raspy breath, very unlike his usual clear, confident voice. Always the optimist, he said he simply had a bad cold. As we talked my gut tightened. I focused on his voice, not what he was saying. He was having difficulty breathing and talking at the same time. He might be worse off than he surmised. At the retirement center, a staff member with medical training was available to him at all times. He promised me he would have his condition evaluated. Several phone calls transpired. Late that evening, he was admitted to the hospital.

Pneumonia. He was diagnosed with pneumonia, the dreaded disease known to be a damnable killer, especially of the elderly.

Day Three

My older sister, Lois, lived in Portland, Oregon, closer to Daddy than I did. Unlike me, she was retired. Fortunately, she was able to arrive the following day. Daddy was regaining his strength; the doctors encouraged us they had caught the pneumonia in time. That good news, coupled with the fact it had been only five weeks since my visit, helped me decide to remain in Denver. Daddy, Lois, and I stayed connected by frequent phone calls. Everyone was rejoicing in his improvement.

Then came Day Three. That morning about eleven o'clock, my dad suffered a severe heart attack. Lois relayed to me the resulting scenario. Hospital staff converged to help and to get him to the Intensive Care Unit. In frantic confusion they careened his hospital bed down the corridor, crashed it into a corner, and ended up on a wrong elevator. Nonetheless, only minutes later, he arrived safely at the ICU in the basement of the hospital. Doctors there confirmed he had had a massive heart attack. He appeared to be dead…but then…he wasn't. Even so, no one expected him to survive more than a few minutes or hours.

But he did. As he explained later, about four o'clock that afternoon, he heard voices in the room. He could feel his fingers, so he flexed them. He opened his eyes, saw Lois's husband Ted, and asked for the newspaper. He remarked, "I haven't done the *Jumble* yet today, have I?"

The hospital was abuzz with wonder. Nurses and doctors paused outside his room to see the "miracle man." Eventually Daddy asked, "Where did I go? Was I dead?"

Carols on a Spring Night

Perhaps he was waiting for me. As quickly as possible, I left home to be with him. No flights were available until mid-morning of the following day, so I drove all night, my own travel a steady course cutting through the emptiness of the long stretches of interstate that comprised the 850-mile journey from Denver to Boise. Interstate 25 north to Fort Collins, the two-lane mountainous Highway 287 shortcut to Laramie, followed by long, straight stretches of I-80 across the high plains of Wyoming. Just me and the semis, where I could exceed the speed limit. My dad had promised to come to my home next Christmas, so it seemed appropriate to listen to carols that night as I sped along, following my headlights through the darkness. Christmas carols resonated in the nighttime of early spring. It was a curiously comforting mix that carried me forward. When I left the interstate, driving the mountainous, twisting Highway 30 into Idaho, it was well past midnight. The combination of the challenging road and the knowledge a deer could dart into my headlights at any moment helped keep me awake. US-30 connected with I-15 south of Pocatello. From there the drive became less challenging: briefly on I-86 and finally onto I-84, which would take me to my dad. I had to traverse the width of the state, but I was on the home stretch.

Pre-dawn light of a new day revealed to me the comforting silhouettes of the familiar low, treeless mountains that led to and formed an arc east and north of Boise. Somehow I found the hospital and abandoned my vehicle in the parking garage across the street. I was thankful, finally, to stretch my legs. I had been thirteen hours at the steering wheel. As I hurried toward the hospital's main entrance, I noted the bountiful blossoms of spring bulbs decorating the grounds. I knew that Daddy, who had always looked forward to the blooming of the cheerful red Emperor tulips he had planted along his driveway, would love to see them. Spring was his favorite time of the year.

Once inside I received directions to his third-floor room. I entered quietly. Tubes. Noise from an apparatus providing the oxygen he was breathing via prongs in his nostrils. I quietly pulled over a chair and sat at his bedside. I gently touched his right hand. It was not my intent to awaken him, but he turned his head toward me, opened his eyes, and said, "Oh, Jean. I'm glad you're here." His tone, neither doleful nor evoking of sympathy, told me the dad I'd always known was still with us.

The Promise

He was stable. In fact, physical therapy was to begin that morning. Unbeknownst to us, this would be the day my father would meet his last new friend. Thirty-something, good-looking, passionate about life, bright, sensitive: this was Mark, Daddy's physical therapist. Their mutual qualities of sincerity and humility, along with their respect for and interest in each other, were readily apparent to everyone. As was his custom, Daddy inquired about Mark's background—where he had grown up, where he had gone to school—these were the usual questions Daddy asked. He loved people and finding connections with them. With Mark, it felt like more than a connection; it was as though they had been friends forever. My dad's first career was as a teacher, but most of his life had been devoted to work with wildlife. Mark's original training was as a fisheries biologist. They shared the same aesthetic regarding the natural world. They were biologists; they knew some of the same people. In addition, Daddy had known people Mark had only read about: Aldo Leopold and Olaus Murie, who, along with my father, were pioneers in wildlife management and environmental causes. My dad was especially animated whenever Mark was around.

Mark spoke sincerely with and listened intently to this man named Levi. At one point, he asked Daddy if he had a favorite food. That is, was there something he craved that probably would not be on his hospital meal tray? Used to an unimaginative diet, Daddy thought for a minute, and replied that he especially liked Fig Newtons and oranges. Mark smiled when Daddy explained how he was able to open an orange so the peeling stayed practically intact. Therefore, none of us was too surprised when on his next visit, Mark brought along a package of Fig Newtons and two oranges. Daddy demonstrated his trademark peeling of an orange and the two savored the flavorful segments.

While they snacked, they talked. Mark said, "I live out in the foothills at the edge of town, close to Hulls Gulch Nature Reserve. Have you been out there?"

"I'm familiar with the general area but haven't been there since it was designated a nature reserve."

"Well, then, you know what it's like. I love its wildness, an easy escape from the city. I go there a lot. Often I'm lucky enough to see one of the great horned owls that live out there."

"Good for you! Those owls are magnificent creatures."

Then came *the promise*. Mark leaned forward in his chair as he said, "When you are stronger, I'll take you to Hulls Gulch and we'll go in search of the owl."

Daddy straightened up. His face lit up as he answered, "I'd love to go." I could almost hear the gears in his head turning as he anticipated being out on a hike, sharing his love of nature with a like-minded adventurer. I could imagine the two of them walking along a dirt path, my dad pointing out buds or birds with his cane and being a tutor to much-younger Mark. Yes, he was ready. It was only his body that was not.

Final Question Number One

Within a couple of days of Mark's promise, our dad was making good progress toward overcoming the pneumonia and recovering from the heart attack. Food tasted good to him again. My dad, my sister Lois, her husband Ted, and I were spending memorable, often fun, times together. My brother, Robert, could not be with us due to job constraints, but he stayed in touch by phone. I was enjoying long, wonderful days at my dad's bedside, watching March Madness basketball games with him and building more memories.

He engaged in conversation with each change of attending personnel. If they woke him to give him his meds, he smiled and thanked them. It was reassuring to observe his flexibility. This was a wise man. I was continuing to learn from him; he was working on continuing the life he loved so much. Or so I thought.

One afternoon, he and I were alone in the room. As was true most of the time, he was in bed. We had been chatting about who-knows-what; Daddy was never at a loss for things to talk about.

He looked at me with his kind brown eyes and asked, "Do you and Lois and Robert still need me?"

The syllables of the monumental question reverberated inside my head. I wanted to shout, "Daddy, we need you more than you will ever know! You are indispensable! I don't know what I'd ever do without you!" However, in that brief instant it took him to finish the question, I knew that was what I *wanted*—for him always to be there. But was it what I *needed*? It was the most difficult question I'd ever encountered. I knew he trusted me to give an honest answer. I responded with what came to me at that moment. I said, "Daddy, we will never stop needing you to receive our love and to love us. You are a wonderful, thoughtful father. But could Lois and Robert and I take care of ourselves and each other without you? I believe we could."

I don't know if there was any one perfect answer to his question, but I hope my answer was comforting to him. I was so unprepared. At a time when I supposed him to be recovering, to be preparing to return to his retirement apartment, he, wisely, was gathering information he could utilize at the imminence of his death.

I have thought about that question time and time again, trying to script the consummate reply. He had asked if we, his three adult children, still needed him. The delineation between need and want has come to mind whenever I have tried to compose another answer. What we needed and what he needed to do could not be in conflict. He needed to give in to his body's failings. How selfish of us if we were to need what he could not provide. Providing for us had always been important to him. I could not let him die thinking he was letting us down. We could *want* him never to leave us. But how could we *need* him never to leave us? Yes, we needed his love. However, I knew even then the love would endure, with or without his physical presence.

I have continued to hope my answer served him well.

The Timepiece

We all have heard it: the story of the grand clock ceasing to function at the time of the owner's death. A timepiece counting off sixty ticks per minute poses a fascinating juxtaposition to the human heart with its usual rhythmic beats. Housed within each of us is an internal clock. Perhaps that internal clock is, in fact, our own heart, accompanying our lives with careful measures of time, counted in well-spaced beats.

In the final days of my dad's life, another version of the clock story was written. It went like this…

My father had never owned a magnificent timepiece. In his apartment was one of those electric clocks that sang a different bird song at each of the twelve hours. A small alarm clock was positioned on his bedside table. He had worn only two wristwatches in all the time I could remember. The first, of which he had been particularly proud, was an Elgin given to him by Mother. The second, a modest watch, was the one he had worn for the last several years. It was on his arm during his hospital stay. One afternoon, he commented the watch was losing time.

We already knew his inner clock, his ninety-four-year-old heart, was faltering. Now even his wrist-born clock had gone awry. The wristwatch was not battery-operated, so a quick fix was not possible. Ted offered to take the watch in to be cleaned or repaired.

Something in me was crying out, not wanting it to be so. The situation was diametrically opposed to the balance and predictability I was needing from life.

None of the other three—my father, Lois, or Ted—evidenced concern about the event. I alone had viewed this happening—the faltering of Dad's watch—as an omen.

Final Question Number Two

I had left home quickly to be with my father when he experienced his severe heart attack. But after a week with him, and given his apparent improving health, I made the decision to return home to Colorado.

Aunt Dolores, his older brother's widow, had died. Leaving early Sunday evening, I could be at her funeral in Nebraska on Tuesday. Obviously my dad could not go. It made sense for my sister to remain with him. While we felt strongly about the importance of having our family represented at Dolores's funeral, an additional factor influenced our decision. It related to what our cousin Ann had told us when she called to inform us of her mom's death.

Ann and Dolores lived together. Her mom had been in failing health, often expressing her readiness to die. In the twenty-four hours before her death she faded out of consciousness and stopped breathing. Ann shook her shoulder, calling her back from what must have been a near-death experience.

In a frail voice, Dolores said, "It's a fabulous fortunate day to see angels in cornfields and chase wild horses with them."

She went on to explain that Phares, her deceased husband, had been there in the Nebraska cornfield with her, along with our mom and dad. Phares and Mom with angels…OK…yes, they were dead and perhaps that was plausible. But she had seen our father also.

My sister and I thought back to the happenings, nearly a thousand miles apart, on the day of our aunt's curious description of her near-death adventure. My face and arms tingled when we realized her experience would have coincided with Dad's heart attack, when doctors, as well as Daddy, thought he had been dead.

We never will understand more than that. However, such a connection begged for me to represent our family at the funeral. Daddy encouraged me to go; he even asked me to sign the guest book on his behalf.

I always will remember one of the last things he asked me before I departed on my long drive. It was a fatherly question. "Do you have good tires on your car?"

I had more than good tires. With down-to-earth values and sensible behaviors modeled by my parents, I was well prepared for my life journey. Good tires equal common sense preparation. Sufficient sleep. Eating a balanced diet. Drinking enough water. Taking vitamins. Honoring nature. Living within one's means. All are akin to *good tires on your car*.

Whenever I tell people about my dad's question, they smile knowingly. Parents care about their children and do whatever they can to look out for them, even well into the child's adult years. My tire story is but one example of a loving lifetime relationship between parent and child.

After I assured him my tires were fine, I promised I would return on Father's Day. I kissed him.

"I love you. Know that I will always be with you."

"I love you, Jean. And I will always be with you, too."

My good tires carried me home safely, as well as to Aunt Dolores's funeral and back. I signed Daddy's name in the guest book as he had requested. We funeral attendees each received a memorial program on which was included Dolores's words about seeing angels in cornfields and chasing wild horses with them.

April 3

The Nebraska trip had been on Tuesday. Wednesday I returned to work, tired, but thankful I had been with my dad again and had represented our family at Dolores's funeral. I spent Thursday, April third, at the quieter-than-I'd-have-preferred photography gallery.

I arrived home about five thirty that evening. I was unlocking the front door when my phone started ringing.

"Hello?"

"It's me." My sister's voice sounded somber. "Daddy and Mother are together again. He died a few minutes ago."

"Oh my God."

"Look, I can't talk now, but I knew you wanted to know right away. I'll call a little later."

"Okay…well, thanks for letting me know."

There was nothing else to say. My voice trailed off.

Lois helped by signing off with, "We'll talk later. I love you."

"Love you too," I mumbled. "Bye."

Dead. He was dead. My dear father was dead.

It was incongruous that the words *my father* would share a sentence with the word *dead*. Dead was an adjective, describing something. How could it apply to my father who had always been so full of life, so ready for the next adventure?

I had called Lois that morning before I left for work. It was then I learned he'd suffered another heart attack. This time it was clear he was dying. Although he was weak and in pain, I was able to speak with him briefly.

"I love you," I said.

"I love you too," I heard him tell me for what would turn out to be the last time.

There had been no need for Lois and me to be in contact unless there was a change in Daddy's condition, so I had waited all day in nauseous anticipation of the next call. Now it had come, but even though I had known the call would come, I was ill prepared for the sobering finality of the news.

I sobbed. I moaned. The unfeeling walls of my home resonated with my screams of primal pain as I tried to escape the undeniable truth. I'd known he was dying, but I still wasn't ready. *He* wasn't ready. He was too young. He was *only* ninety-four.

I didn't want to hear the questions hammering inside my head, much less pretend to know the answers. Numb, helpless, and ever so alone, there was nothing to do but cry. So I cried. But the company of my outcries brought me no solace. In longing and desperation, I called out for my father. In the quiet that followed, there was no answer.

The person I longed to talk to was Daddy. That being impossible, I desperately wanted to be in touch with my only child, my daughter, Mindy. I'd been single since she was nine. However, she and her husband were away on a short but long-anticipated cruise; it would serve only my own needs to contact her on the high seas with this sad news. I knew I must wait three days to talk with her. Besides, only a few days ago, Daddy had mentioned their trip. He was aware of how much they were looking forward to it. I was convinced he would not have wanted it interrupted.

My thoughts alternated between welcome, stabilizing memories of my dad, and overpowering visions associated with the chasmic concept of his death. The evening seemed endless. More phone calls transpired, most of which I scarcely remember. Eventually my dismal spirit was camouflaged, surrounded by the ebony darkness of night.

So began life without my dad. Although I was not yet aware of it, my solitary *search for the owl,* an emotional sojourn that was to last one year, had already begun.

Preparations

In the days immediately following the news of Daddy's death, grieving was counterbalanced by countless demanding decisions that could not be postponed. Throughout those days, time warped, either flying by or heavy and slow with difficult emotion.

Other family members and I needed to make travel arrangements. Knowing I would want to bring home many things, I made plans to drive yet again the familiar route to what had been my childhood home. However, this trip felt far different. For the first time in my life, no parent would be waiting at the other end.

There would be two services. The first would take place at our dad's church in Boise, the city that had been home to him for almost fifty years. The other would be five days later in Wauneta, the small Nebraska town near his birthplace. He would be buried in the rural cemetery beside Mother, not far from where they'd been high school sweethearts.

There were issues regarding the obituary, ministers, legal matters, and flowers. Daddy's suit needed to be dry cleaned. What tie should he have on? There were also simpler tasks such as stopping delivery of his newspaper and retrieving his watch from the repair shop. The entire process seemed too bizarre to be real. Unfortunately, it was all *too* real. On and on, one resolution after another led us closer to what would be the time of ultimate physical closure: the burial of our dad's body.

It helped that my sister, brother, and I were of like minds regarding most arrangements. Emotionally, we supported each other the best we could. (After all, I had promised Daddy we would be OK without him.) I felt grateful the writing of the obituary fell to me. I included details my dad had reviewed with me only days before his death. I believe he had known he was dying and wanted others to be reminded of facets of his life he considered important.

The First Service

The week following his death provided the opportunity for my siblings and me to begin processing our loss. Time shared with family members who came together from across the country was precious. I was thankful my daughter, Mindy, and her husband, Adam—now returned from their cruise—were able to come from Colorado for the funeral.

Daddy's six great-grandchildren played tirelessly, hiding behind our chairs and engaging in other antics. We welcomed the laughter and endless energy from those descendants who were too young to fathom the depth of the loss the rest of us were experiencing.

The service at Daddy's church was on Friday afternoon, eight days after his death. I was touched by the profusion of floral arrangements that had been sent to honor him. The pews in the enormous sanctuary were almost half full, a tribute to the number of lives he had touched. The service was lovely. My sister had masterfully pulled together pictures for a video depiction of Daddy's life. I was thankful the remarks by the minister sounded like he was talking about my dad, as opposed to some services I have attended where I've scarcely recognized the individual in the speaker's comments. Among the hymns we had chosen to sing was, "This Is My Father's World." For me, the lyrics "in the rustling grass I hear

Him pass, He speaks to me everywhere" took on a welcome double meaning.

I planned to listen.

At the reception following the funeral, we displayed small items from nature. In the twenty-four hours preceding the service, relatives had contributed whatever they deemed appropriate. I collected several velvety curling seedpods from a locust tree. Others gathered bird feathers, chunks of creviced bark, smooth speckled rocks from the Boise River, and other specimens. These were contained in a large rectangular glass box on a metal stand. Many things flowed out onto the table. Daddy had loved calling our attention to the intricate beauty of these small wonders, so this display served as a fitting tribute to him.

Daddy's relatives, friends, and acquaintances offered recollections and kind words to us, his three children.

A hug. Then, "Your parents were great neighbors all those years when we lived next door on Michael Street. We loved the way your dad kept those rose bushes blooming profusely."

"Thanks. Yes, he loved cutting a bouquet or even a single perfect rosebud to bring in for Mom. Thanks so much for being here today."

Next, "I always admired your dad when we worked together at the Fish and Game Department. We all appreciated his thoroughness whether analyzing an issue or designing a response or new project."

"That's good to hear. It means a lot."

"And…he was every inch a gentleman."

"So true. We three were fortunate to have him for our father."

On and on it went: warm handshakes, hugs, and additional reassuring words—an outpouring of warmth and love.

We encouraged everyone to take an item from our nature display. It was gratifying to observe the care with which each person selected a delicate feather, a twisted seedpod, or perhaps a twig with evenly spaced berries—a treasure to carry home as a remembrance of our dad.

At the family dinner afterward, I distributed the invitations for Christmas at my home more than eight months in the future. I had planned to mail them in April. It now was April. My dad had suggested that gathering. Due to a combination of factors, he had not been to my home for Christmas for thirty years. During that time, it had become a tradition for Mom and Dad to spend the holiday at Lois and Ted's. I had started preparing for the event before he was hospitalized, including writing the save-the-date invitations. I had wanted everyone to plan ahead for Christmas at my house with Daddy and the rest of the family. Of course, I had prepared an invitation for Daddy as well. What should I do with it? After adding Mom's name, I requested the funeral home director place it in the inner pocket of Daddy's suit coat, close to his heart.

By midday Saturday, the day after the funeral, everyone had headed home except Lois, Ted, and me. We spent the rest of the day with miscellaneous tasks, including preparing Daddy's apartment to be unoccupied until Lois could return and arrange to have things moved to storage. Final sorting and decisions about our dad's belongings would need to wait a few months until we three siblings could come together to devote time and attention to that task.

As we worked, Lois, Ted, and I were looking forward to eight thirty the next morning. What Mark had promised to do with Daddy, he had agreed to do with us. He was taking us to Hulls Gulch in search of the owl.

Hulls Gulch

Sunday morning the weather was cool but pleasant. Only Mark was familiar with the irregular streets on this side of town, so I rode in his small vehicle from our rendezvous spot and Lois and Ted followed in theirs. There was plenty of room in the parking lot at the wilderness area. We set out along the wide path, eager to begin our search. Giant cottonwoods stood watch over us; the thick undergrowth was partially dormant. It was obvious from the many nests in evidence and the surround-sound of songs and calls that this was a haven for birds. We chatted about Daddy and agreed he would have been delighted with this adventure. I would have preferred a quieter, more contemplative experience, but that is difficult with four people. As we explored, we were looking intently for the owl, pointing to an occasional large bird in flight and combing the trees with our eyes. We chose the longest loop, one that covered most of the gulch wilderness. However, even with four pairs of eyes, we failed to manage a glimpse of the owl.

We returned to our vehicles. Lois and Ted left; I would connect with them later in the day. Mark drove me back to my car. He was aware of how disappointed I was in not seeing the owl and how heavy-hearted I was. He was comfortable with my crying. It felt safe and good to cry with Mark, my dad's last new friend. I thanked him for his positive role in Daddy's last days and for attending the services on Friday. We hugged, said our good-byes, and promised to keep in touch.

    I got into my car. Mark drove away. How should I spend my next few hours? I needed to depart later in the day to drive the first leg of my journey home. But something told me that before leaving, I needed to go back to Hulls Gulch…alone.

Revisiting Hulls Gulch

The sky turned overcast and the air developed a distinct chill. A warmer coat would have been great, but I began my walk anyway. I was surprised at how much more I noticed when I was alone. I heard more birds; I noticed the profusion of orange lichen on the rough tree bark. I was grateful I had decided to return. This search felt more purposeful. Again, I chose the long route, looping around the tallest cottonwood. Although I looked everywhere, my search was in vain. A light rain began. Disappointed once more, I lifted the hood of my lightweight windbreaker and headed back.

At the crossover point of the long and short trails, I met a jovial older couple. In contrast to my minimal outerwear, they had on rainproof headgear and substantial jackets. We exchanged greetings. I perked up, commenting on what a splendid retreat this was and informing them today had been my first visit. The two told me they frequented the area. The man asked, "Did you see the owl?"

My heart skipped a beat. I scarcely could believe what I had heard!

I said, "No, but I would like to," trying to control my incredible excitement.

"We'll go back with you."

"If you don't mind, yes, that would be great." Not wanting to disrupt the serendipity of the moment, I decided to keep to myself the true nature of my quest.

We walked quietly back along the trail. We stopped at the tall cottonwood I had circled only minutes earlier from the opposite direction. They pointed at a branch fifteen feet above the ground. There sat the sought-after great horned owl. I watched it for several seconds, not wanting to miss this experience in the event it flew away. I thanked them. They left.

The drizzle continued but I was no longer cold. The owl, perched close to the solid trunk on a strong branch of this aged tree, was camouflaged against the dappled bark. We watched each other intently. It felt magical...too good to be real. A great horned owl is a sizeable creature about twenty inches tall, at once magnificent and ordinary. I could see this one well and attempted to memorize its salient features: huge yellow eyes, tufts of feathers that protruded like horns, striped markings, a wide curved beak, and strong talons. It was striking.

But also, it was quiet, possessing what struck me as the epitome of aplomb. Keenly observant, it tilted or twisted its head to listen. Or was it to see? Its eyes were all-knowing and virtually piercing with their intensity. Even when its head rotated on its swivel base, it could still see me. The owl cocked its head to one side. Was it to scrutinize or to communicate? Then, the beautiful creature blinked, as though to add, "Amen," to a pearl of wisdom.

The tranquil nature of this powerful symbol of wisdom surprised me. This owl had not been readily observed, was not clamoring for attention. Not *doing* anything, it simply *was*.

I stepped closer to the tree. The owl remained perched, observing me. I spoke quietly, thanking it for appearing, acknowledging its splendor. Eventually there seemed to be nothing more I could do. My experience felt complete.

I returned to my car with thankfulness and amazement welling within me. I had seen an owl...the owl my father had anticipated searching for in the final days of his life. My search for clues to the mystery of life and death, that ongoing, unpredictable adventure dubbed the *search for the owl*, had begun to unfold.

The Next Steps

It was late afternoon by the time I was ready to begin my three hundred mile drive to Soda Springs. Before I left, Lois dug a clump of white violets from beside Daddy's patio for me to take home. On the floor of the passenger side of my car, I secured the Easter lily that had been sent by friends of mine for Daddy's services. I positioned the large glass display box, still holding a piece of rough bark and a locust pod, in a protected spot on the back seat. Along with the plants and the box, I loaded my car with belongings that had been Mother and Daddy's: two oak straight-back chairs, the teddy bears I had given each of them (Mom's had been snuggled against her when she died), and a flowerpot with one of Mom's African violets that Lois and Daddy had kept alive since her death. I also took Daddy's fancy purple and gold King of Hearts crown.

I drove out the circular driveway of the retirement home. Out of habit, I glanced back. But this time, my dad was not there waving to me. Once again, with a lump in my throat and tears in my eyes, I drove away.

The several-hour drive provided the alone time I craved, the opportunity to reflect and to process all that had happened and was continuing to happen. The miles slipped by.

It was well after sundown when I arrived at my destination for the night, desperately tired and carrying the weight of a profound sadness.

Searching Again

Upon awakening, I noted it was light outside. I heard a train wail in the distance. I glanced at the clock. It was after eight. I lay still, savoring the welcome morning solitude, readying myself mentally for the long day ahead before I would reach the solace of home.

I had spent the night at the Caribou Lodge, owned by friends whom I had come to know over the course of scores of road trips back and forth to visit Mom and Dad, and later, Dad. Daddy and I had stayed there on one of our trips. They insisted I eat breakfast with them; I welcomed their thoughtful gesture. As I ate my cereal and enjoyed their strong coffee, we talked, and intermittently I cried. They stopped eating and listened quietly as I told my story of seeing the great horned owl. It was comforting to have this oasis of hospitality and compassion before the final leg of my drive home.

After breakfast I was in no hurry to go, but knew I must. I was scheduled to work the next day. The following day I would drive to Nebraska for Daddy's final services and burial. Yes, I needed to leave. I said good-bye and headed east. I drove considerably below the speed limit until I reached the state line, hesitant to leave the state where my dad had lived and died. After I crossed the border, I increased my speed, intent upon hastening the passage of miles and perhaps time. An immeasurable melancholy continued to fill my being.

I was thankful for another chance to reflect on the past weeks, to feel the enormity of the void in my life, and to explore the fullness of my emotions. Symbolically, the distant horizons provided ample space for it all. Each time I sighted an antelope on the wide-open plains, I experienced a brief but welcome surge of joy.

On an earlier trip to visit my dad, I had seen fluffy fledgling owls in Sinclair, Wyoming, a tiny town that lay ahead. They had been perched in a flower box nest on a second-story window of a vacant hotel. Although the interstate bypassed the town, its quaint town square and numerous trees provided a change from the wide-open sagebrush desert, so I often detoured through there for a change of pace, adding a mere five minutes to my trip. I needed to see if owls were anywhere in evidence today. I'd had the good fortune to see a great horned owl yesterday. I could not imagine I would be lucky enough to see another one, but the possibility intrigued me and it was worth the stop.

I parked in front of the hotel with its padlocked front door and sagging Venetian blinds. The street was empty. I craned my neck and shaded my eyes to look at the lofty window box. Nothing. I scanned the rooflines of the hotel and the adjacent buildings. No owls. No birds at all.

In the wide grassy median loomed a majestic spruce, nearly forty feet tall. I crossed the street and approached the tree. Its dense, healthy growth habit and numerous branches made it difficult to see through to the trunk. I assumed if an owl were there, it would be toward the interior, close to where the branches joined the trunk. I sidestepped from one spot to another, moving to wherever I could see into the shaded depths of the conifer.

After less than a minute of searching, I saw it. A great horned owl was perched two-thirds of the way up the tree, close to the stout trunk. My heart quickened. I was dumbfounded. I was overjoyed. I wavered between believing this was a bird and this was a spiritual presence. Perhaps it was both. I stood transfixed, making the experience a part of every cell of my being. It watched. I watched.

I slowly raised my arm, inviting the magnificent being to land on my coat sleeve. It remained quiet. I spoke softly, again expressing gratitude for its presence. I moved slowly to other vantage points, hoping for a more unobstructed view while continuing to savor the experience. I don't know how long the owl and I stayed there beholding each other. All concept of time disappeared. Eventually, hesitatingly, not knowing what else to do, I whispered good-bye. I floated back to my vehicle, climbed in, and drove away.

The remainder of the drive home seemed far easier. It was clear my quest was resulting in serendipitous discoveries. I believed I would be guided toward a deeper understanding of life...and death.

Home Again

At home, another huge stack of mail confronted me. I sorted it into four piles: bills, sympathy cards and other personal correspondence, junk mail, and items belonging to that grey-area-in-between. This time I had been away eight days. Earlier, I had been gone seven days when I went to spend time with Daddy. Between the two trips, I was home only a few days. It was no wonder I was disoriented and exhausted. Now I would be here one day before the long day of travel to Nebraska for the services and burial, and the final drive home.

I now had two stacks of mail categorized as the grey-area-in-between. The first, from my earlier absence, waited for me right where I had sorted it several days ago. After opening the new bills and correspondence and unpacking a few toiletries, I collapsed into bed.

Today I Buried My Dad

At my dad's service in Wauneta, I spoke briefly to the handful of people who honored him by their presence. Time at his graveside and the finality of his burial were extremely difficult for me. I drove home late that evening not only by myself, but utterly alone. Before midnight, exhausted as I was, I took a few minutes to capture the essence of the day.

> Today I buried my dad. Today was my dad's funeral. Today, I viewed my dad's remains for the last time. Soon, this will have happened yesterday, then, last week, and all too soon, last year. Today. I want to hold onto this day, to relive it all while it's still today. The strength of the powerful wind sending tumbleweeds dancing in cornfields. The wild white clouds scooting across the blue sky. The Nebraska bouquet on his casket with its ears of seed-corn. My convulsive sobbing at graveside. Moments of laughter. The joyful reassurance of sighting the redwinged blackbird and the cock pheasant...

Changes

I wanted to digest what had happened before I was consumed by the busyness of life. I needed more time to experience the precious memories and the cavernous feelings of loss. I sensed it was unusual *not* to long for the passage of time in hopes of more quickly getting to where I could feel *normal* again.

Of course, there was no normalcy to which to retreat. Neither I nor my world would ever be the same. That is not to say I would grieve for the rest of my days or I would never experience extended happiness. No. That I would not be the same was a statement of truth. It was not value-laden. I did not believe I necessarily would be any better or worse than before. Rather, I would be different, because of the inherently life-changing experience of losing a parent whom I had loved so dearly.

The Trial

A few days after my dad's burial, I reported for jury duty. I had postponed my appearance once, so this time it was mandatory. Emotionally fragile and sleep-deprived, I checked in along with 249 of my fellow citizens to fulfill my civic responsibility. Under other circumstances, participation would have been fine, even welcome as a learning experience. However, in my current state, I did not relish the idea. I did not trust my behavior in such an unfeeling, austere environment.

I chose a seat in the large room as far away as possible from the chatter of the TVs. Jurors were to be selected for three trials that morning: two criminal, one civil. We waited for more than an hour. There were periodic announcements. Finally, random selection of groups of forty-five jurors began. That meant nearly half of us soon would be free to leave.

I was aware of someone calling my name and saying…"is number ten. Please come forward and take a green juror tag." Oh, no. This was not how it was supposed to happen. I had anticipated being back home by noon.

Sometime later the announcement was made that parties in two of the three cases had settled out of court. Which group of jurors needed to stay? Of course, it was those of us with the green tags. The other potential jurors gathered their belongings and left. I remained with the others who also sported the lucky-colored tags.

The process involved waiting more than anything else. Finally in late morning we were escorted to an upstairs courtroom. The young Black defendant and his Hispanic attorney were seated at one table; a sharply dressed Anglo district attorney sat at the other. The defendant leaned forward, hands tightly clasped, eyes cast downward. We learned the criminal trial we had drawn involved an assault with a deadly weapon. Aware that an inordinate number of male youths of color become entangled in our judicial system, I wanted to provide a sensitive ear, but I was not sure I could be there for him.

From the jury pool, thirteen were to be selected for the trial: twelve jurors and one alternate. The judge asked questions to which we responded by raising a hand or not. He asked if there were circumstances that would make it difficult or impossible for us to complete the expected five-day trial. I inched my hand up. When it was my turn, I explained that my father had died recently. I described the emotional fragility I was experiencing and my concern as to how well I could focus on the proceedings. I assured them I honestly did not know how it would be for me. I was surprised at how weak my voice sounded, evidence of the truth of my words. Although I tried to sound matter-of-fact, I'm certain those listening could tell my emotions hovered close to the surface. As I spoke, the room became quiet. Amidst concerns about childcare or important doctor appointments or plane reservations, my comments cut to a core to which others were sensitive. I was thankful my voice was not breaking. It was an unlikely place to be talking about my father's death: in a courtroom preceding a criminal trial. As I left the courtroom midday for our lunch break, a female guard complimented me on my multi-colored scarf. I believe she had heard my story and wanted to offer me her gift of kind words.

While in the courthouse lunchroom, I was surprised to receive several expressions of sympathy from total strangers who had been brought together for this trial. That anyone had separated my small voice from the issues and questions that filled the courtroom was affirmation of the honesty of my expression.

I managed to down a bland roast beef sandwich and bottle of apple juice. After lunch, we returned to the courtroom. The judge continued with his questions. Other jurors were dismissed. It was time for questions by the defense attorney and district attorney. I was exhausted. At times, I found myself holding my head in my hands. I was having difficulty concentrating on the courtroom proceedings. I was asked again to state my concerns regarding availability for the trial. I rephrased my earlier remarks, and added, "My dad and I were very close. I miss him." It was a private, intimate disclosure revealed in an unfeeling public place. Why was it happening this way? Why was my grief becoming part of a court record?

I will never know. I was dismissed later that afternoon.

Loss

Death of a loved one brings about the ultimate loss of control for those who are left behind. There is no way to change the outcome, no way to bring them back. There is nothing to do but to let go of the one who has died. As difficult as it would be, I needed to attempt to let go of my father and the need for excessive control in my day-to-day existence.

During that time I also experienced a loss of control in my finances. Reduced income related to uncompensated time away from work, coupled with unexpected expenses, knocked my budget out of kilter. Although frustration over money was a minor irritation compared to all-consuming sorrow and the finality of death, it was one more issue to confront when one more was one too many. It was an additional burden, cruel and unfair.

Loss of routine. Unavoidable neglect of so much. How was I to re-order my life when priorities had become so skewed? How was I to get back to…? But no, there was no going back, only ahead: picking up pieces, combining them with memories and whatever else I might find along the way to create something new.

Metaphor

Interwoven amongst the darkness of grief and the bright moments of joy, between nagging misgivings and gratitude for new awakenings, were the golden threads of my *search for the owl*. My quest was neither something to be accomplished nor a destination; rather, it was a journey. I had seen owls on two consecutive days. I had experienced something my dad had been anticipating in his final days. Yes, the serendipitous experiencing of the owls so soon after my dad died provided a sense of deep satisfaction.

In search of the owl became a metaphor for my sojourn to discover clues that would lead to a deeper understanding of life. Of course, it wasn't about finding an owl at all. It was about seeking wisdom via vital lessons I needed to learn on my own.

Tiny Wonders

My dad had loved watching wildlife. He was in awe of the grand scheme of nature. But perhaps even more, he had reveled in its tiny wonders. With the box of elements from nature at his funeral, we acknowledged that appreciation. From the time I can remember, he had pointed out the jigsaw-puzzle patterning of the bark of the ponderosa pine, the complex flowers of the early-blooming maple, the gentle beauty of a pastel sunset, and other miracles of nature.

Therefore, it was natural the things that comforted me and brought a smile to my often tear-streaked face were aspects of nature I observed: the delicate yet intensely colored blossoms on the redbud tree across the street, the purplish stain of the aspen catkins on the wet sidewalk, and yes, the subtle maple flowers decorating the tree outside my front door. Nature's gifts, both grandiose and miniscule; I gave thanks for every one.

One Week

It was late evening and I was journaling again.

>Today marks one week since my father's burial and my desperate, late-night scribbling. All too soon it will not be this month, but last month, that my father died. The urgency of translating feelings, thoughts, and memories into words is compelling. This writing cannot be done later. It must be done now, while tears blur the words. It must be done while the tiny seed of inkling can be nurtured by expanding it into words and letting it be watered by those same tears. Thus, perhaps it can grow into something more easily understood, for sometimes the hand writes what the heart commands.

Focus

With the *search for the owl* as my private adventure, focus on the quest became intense and virtually automatic. Similar to the way newly discovered love creates excitement and an altered sense of awareness, my search brought an attitude of anticipation that accompanied my deep feeling of loss. A thick lens of emotion focused my awareness on the *now* so it grew impossible to miss the precious essence of the moment.

During this time of ongoing melancholy, the entire surface of my skin felt tense as if ready to receive information important to my search. Because I believed cues could be derived through all of my senses, I maintained an air of openness and expectation.

Once Is Not Enough

Another late evening. Writing had become a nightly obsession since my father died. I was driven by my desire to attach words to my feelings and to capture my questions as I sought answers.

Not only was there no new insight today, for the first time since Daddy's funeral, there was not one sympathy card in my mailbox. So again, I immerse myself in my writing.

My belief is strong that valuable clues about life and, perhaps, life after this life will appear. Balancing my feeling of loss is a spiritual burgeoning, nurtured by the reawakening world of spring.

Earlier today my eyes fell upon the printed words on a plastic bag. Encouraging recycling, they read, ONCE IS NOT ENOUGH. Was it serendipity I noticed and paid attention to those words? Were they hinting at a grander sense of recycling? I must continue my journey while pondering the concept once is not enough.

I read what I had written. It sounded positive. But was I fooling myself through my writing, pretending to be stronger than the tears-just-below-the-surface individual I'd been for the last several days?

Road Signs

The next morning I awoke more rested than I had been for several days. I ate a decent breakfast and was feeling confident about handling my day.

Then on my drive to work, I saw it. The sign read *ROUGH ROAD*. Rough road ahead. I feared it was a warning about my day. In the past weeks I had been on a rough road, a winding road, a steep road, and ever so many other kinds of streets and byways. Emotionally, I had been down roads with harrowing hairpin curves. Life was unfolding like one unending detour. At times I even thought I had reached a dead end. I did not welcome another rough road.

As the day unfurled I learned the *ROUGH ROAD* sign had not been an omen, but a chance to recall what I already had been through. My thoughts about the phrase on the plastic bag and my reaction to the words on the diamond-shaped road sign were examples of the novel interpretations I found myself applying to the otherwise mundane.

Listening

Listening was the theme for the rest of that day: listening on the part of a dear co-worker, my own listening to the call of a crow, and finally, listening to another message from nature.

A trusted, non-judgmental listener is a blessing. That was one role my dad had played for me and it was something I sought out following his death. Therefore, one day I was especially thankful to be working with a quiet-mannered volunteer whom I had not seen for several weeks. As I informed her of my dad's death, tears filled her eyes. She told me that although she had never met him, it was as though she knew him because of the stories I had told her. She recounted for me what I had shared with her about the evening walk my father and I had taken only weeks before his death. There it was again, the importance of telling our stories. I was thankful my friend had reminded me of that special one. After recollections of time with my dad, the rest of the workday passed more quickly.

That evening I chose to drive a different route home. I had become better at listening to myself and to whatever was guiding me, so when I was drawn to a park less than two miles from my home, I paid attention. I had taken Daddy there when it was new. Perhaps because of the walk-in-the-park story, I felt an urge to return. The evening was brisk, much like the one in February. With an air of anticipation, I strolled along the entry sidewalk. What had drawn me here? Which way should I go and what should I explore?

The answer to my last questions was delivered almost immediately. From a perch high overhead on a gracefully curving lamppost, a gleaming black crow called to me. Once certain I was paying attention, the large bird set off in a wide, sweeping circle ahead and to my left. Cawing and gliding, my newfound guide retraced the circle, and then alighted behind me. Now I knew what to do. I had received my instructions: explore the area that had been demarcated for me.

I climbed to an elevated observation deck within that circle, beside a magnificent tree. I sensed an emotional connection with this mature willow. Its gnarled, multi-trunk form contrasted with its graceful branches. Tender spring leaves and drooping willow-catkins decorated its swaying arms. My eyes traveled along its rough bark and the twists of its trunk and branches, traced its outline, searched the ground below, and explored the tiny gurgling waterway nearby that fed this ancient being. Tranquility and grace…I could literally taste the fresh, sweet air. In this long-lived tree was the embodiment of the cycle of life and death—the soft virgin growth patterned against the weathered bark—the catkins ready to produce new life, and below, layers of long-ago-shed leaves. I felt welcomed, sheltered, protected. The message was clear: return again to this place of beauty and the embodiment of strength. Return often. Allow yourself to be nurtured here.

In Black

My emotions fluctuated not only from day to day but from hour to hour and minute to minute. Soon after my uplifting discovery of the ancient willow, I was especially down. Early that afternoon I wrote:

> Clad in black, more inside than out. That is how it is for me now. The grief process is extraordinarily painful when love has been so dearly given and received. Our western society does little to respect or protect one who is grieving. A formal mourning time, recognized by some religions and cultures, is uncommon. The aggressive driver and the impatient customer know nothing of my emotional fragility. I carry no sign other than my tired eyes. My attire is ordinary. I long for the identity and subsequent insulation a black dress and veil would provide. I consider the idea of a black armband.

Wearing such would be an indication I am going through a sensitive time.

I think of the pregnant woman with her engorged belly. Others readily can perceive her condition, her need for a seat on the bus, the importance of not poking her with a package in the elevator. We who are sorrowful would benefit by such a signal to others.

I have now counted nine days since my dad's burial. My heart is laden with a quiet sadness. I am weary. Though I put one foot ahead of the other, it seems I am getting nowhere. I imagine myself as a gentle deer in the forest depths, tired or ill. What would the wild creature do? Retreat to a quiet haven of safety.

So, with much of the business of life waiting, I closed my bedroom door, muted the phone, curled up under the comfortable coverings of my familiar bed, and attempted to sleep.

I was thankful for a cozy place to rest. Mentally I revisited the many expressions of caring and sympathy from others; they offered welcome consolation. I lay still and expressed my gratitude in quiet prayer-like thought. I gave thanks for my wise, loving father and for the shelter not only of my house, but also of that afforded by my small but reliable income. I was grateful for family and friends on whom I knew I could lean. Comforted by these thoughts, I was able to sleep.

When I awoke, it was late afternoon. Refreshed and with a more positive attitude, I was ready to tackle a few household jobs. I had plenty to choose from. In the previous several days, I had been kind to myself, giving priority to good nutrition and rest and addressing only small, manageable tasks.

I wanted to inventory my dad's diaries, several boxfuls in my temporary custody. He had kept a diary for one year when he was eleven years old. His daily writing resumed seventeen years later and continued until his hospitalization a matter of days before his death. The process of writing modeled for me throughout my formative years had become instinctual for me as well.

The diaries were mostly compact, squat books each with five years' worth of notes. Some covered only one or two years. The majority had a tab with a little lock. The tab was often broken off, not from being locked but from the repetitive opening and closing of the diary. What they had in common was inside: words in my dad's familiar scrawling handwriting, words that had captured forever his attention to detail, his positive outlook, his love of family, and his affinity for nature.

I attempted to focus on the goal of noting the years represented by the diary writings. I needed to ascertain all of the diaries were accounted for. Yet I could not resist the temptation to peek inside, to peruse some of the pages, to follow the closely spaced lines of his writing with my eyes, and to listen to my dad's words.

I opened a random volume to read…to listen to my dad. He was speaking of his bright Emperor tulips blooming along the front driveway, of the Audubon banquet he and Mom had attended, and of a phone call from Robert. As I read, rather than sorrow, I experienced reassurance; much of my dad remained through his writing. I could listen to him anytime by reading his words.

In Touch

Not only did my dad journal, but he also utilized the written word to stay in contact with others. While this was especially true with regard to his three children, he also valued frequent communication with his brother, his adult grandchildren, and the sister-in-law who had preceded him in death by only days. He exchanged letters with a wide group of friends. Several times a week, he had walked from his retirement apartment to a nearby care facility to visit another sister-in-law who suffered from dementia. Her death came a few months before his. Any one of us was delighted whenever the mailbox held a handwritten postcard or letter from him. Yes, Daddy loved to write. I treasure the last written communication I received from him: a picture postcard, dated thirteen days before the onset of his bout with pneumonia. The image showed adventuresome river-rafters on a whitewater mountain stream. Instead of "Dear Jean," his handwritten greeting read, "Dear Adventurer," a nod not only to the image but also to *our* many adventures.

I was also glad when the phone rang and I heard his cheerful voice. His calls to me, some as late as eleven at night, always began, "Hello, Jean. This is your dad."

His promise to be in touch with me after he died was one reason for my urgency to go *in search of the owl*, being ever-watchful for indications of his contact. I was aware of the possibility of his presence anywhere and everywhere. Although I did not know how I would experience it, I waited in curious anticipation. Perhaps my dad already had been in touch with me. *Had* the second owl been a spiritual presence? This was all new to me, so I wasn't sure.

The Song

My schedule stayed full. Finally I had another day without early morning commitments, a chance to get some extra sleep. However, I had set my clock radio in case I slept too long. I could ill afford to miss too much of the day.

At eight I was awakened by music from my favorite country station. As I lay in bed looking ahead to the new day, the poignant lyrics of "I'm Already There" seemed directed at me. I listened as the song assured me that *he* was already with me: in the sunshine, in the shadows, and in the moonlight. I was encouraged to listen to *him* in my heartbeat and in the whispering wind. Then the promise: we would always be together.

I turned off the radio and closed my eyes. Of course, I remembered the hymn we had sung with the verse about *the rustling grass* and *hearing Him everywhere*. This unexpected early morning message echoed within me, fostering joyful, wondrous warmth. This time, disguised as Lonestar, either my dad or the owl had sung to me.

A Second Visit

Three weeks had passed since the Sunday I had last seen my father alive. I arose at dawn to allow for a return in early morn to the solace of the newly discovered willow tree. I was experiencing a heightened sensitivity to my *search for the owl*.

The park was deserted, so my visit could be quiet and meditative. As I approached the elevated wooden walkway that led to the deck beside the willow, I observed at my feet the twinkle of frost adorning diagonal stripes of light and shadow, stripes formed by early morning sunlight and the shadows of the vertical slats of the footbridge sides.

The sight brought to mind another time of ice and shadow: it was on an early morning winter outing with Daddy at the MK Nature Center in Boise. That day, after we had noted the proliferation and variety of berries on the shrubs and trees, we had come to a footbridge, slippery with frost and decorated with shadows. We had helped each other across.

This time I was alone. Dare I footprint the delicate ice-patterns nature had created? The willow beckoned, so I moved on, stepping gingerly yet with purpose so as not to slip. Once at the large deck, I leaned against the wet railing...the sunshine had already melted the frost. I listened and looked, savoring my time in the company of nature. I waited. Watching. Wondering. No creatures were in evidence. Suddenly, a squirrel skittered along the rough bark of the willow. In mere seconds, there appeared another, and yet another. Spying me, they halted and studied me curiously. Once satisfied I was *friend*, they continued their game of tag, leaping playfully from branch to branch.

I was buoyed by the antics of the trio of four-legged furry friends. I was thankful for having returned to this place I had come to love and for having waited patiently until these creatures chose to reveal themselves.

It was particularly meaningful to me that I discovered squirrels that morning. Did these three somehow know my dad had befriended one of their kind at his retirement apartment? He had fed a female squirrel by scattering cashews on his patio, eventually placing a trail of the tempting morsels across the threshold of the sliding door and on into his living room. She had become a frequent visitor inside his apartment to retrieve those treats.

The morning the minister, my sister, and I gathered in Daddy's apartment to plan his funeral service, the squirrel showed up outside, unaware my father had died. My sister opened a can of nuts, slowly slid the door open, scattered a few cashews on the carpet, and returned to her chair. We humans sat silently. Our reward was to see the squirrel not only tiptoe inside to collect the treats, but also sit on her haunches in the room to consume them.

When my recollections were complete, it was time to bid farewell to the squirrels and to leave the presence of my new friend the willow. I retraced my footsteps. The footbridge was no longer slick with frost for the April sun was climbing the eastern sky, beaming with the promise of a perfect day.

Emotional Meanderings

After my visit to the park, I went to church and joined the singles group for brunch. I had attended the brunch many times and was looking forward to reconnecting. But I was not ready for casual, much less flirtatious, interactions. An experience I had enjoyed and handled confidently in the past was now foreign territory.

What was disconcerting and foreign? Everything. It is said, "When one thing changes, everything changes." Having lost my second parent, I was not the same person anymore. I was experiencing fear and vulnerability, feelings my adult self had believed were gone forever. Now, having been sublimated for decades, they had resurfaced.

By the time I returned home it was mid-afternoon. My early rising had caught up with me. My energy was depleted. After one realistic look at the dishes in the sink, clutter everywhere, and thick dust on my furniture, I was overwhelmed. Journaling, observing nature, and writing thank-you notes for expressions of sympathy had kept me focused and balanced during my time at home. Now, rather than satisfied with those accomplishments, I was disgusted with myself for what I had *not* done. Scattered, almost nauseous, the melancholy, insecure me began to cry.

As evening approached, the sky turned ominous. Wind rattled the windows. I heard the growl of thunder. Alone, tired, and sad, I crawled into bed, my body tense and cold in the darkening room. My eyelids, wet from an hour's worth of tears, were swollen. Why was I so awkward and ugly?

Then there came a curious, comforting thought: the owl, with its night vision, could be observing me. The concept of my owl was akin to God taking care of me, silently watching, and quietly being there for me. Perhaps, again, I had found the owl.

Not right away, but eventually, I slept.

Wonder

The phrase *in search of the owl* stayed with me no matter what I did or where I went. The haunting quality of it was pleasing. It created within me a sense of wonder.

Infused by this sense of wonder, I inched forward. Sometimes I leapt forward and sometimes I crawled backward. Sometimes I needed to hide. I tried to accept it all, for wherever I found myself, *wondering* had become second nature. Wonderment: sometimes inspiring, other times creating a cavern of utter darkness. It produced questions that cycled toward more learning, which fed the curiosity that fueled the *search for the owl.*

I became obsessed by one question about death. It was, "Why?" Since no one knew, I searched for answers in my own way.

Realizing I might never know did not deter me in my quest… for perhaps I could acquire, if not the answer to that singular question, at least the wise knowingness of the owl.

If it had Been Different

In addition to the *why* of death, I also wondered about the *how* of my dad's death: pneumonia. The stress of pneumonia on his body had contributed to two heart attacks. Within twelve days, the person I knew as my dad had been transformed from an energetically alive being into a silent, lifeless body, best described by the word *dead*. I agonized over his way of dying, wishing it had been different. How unfair for life to have been snatched from my vibrant father. Why couldn't he have died without enduring that final suffering? Preceding his final heart attack, he had spent the last night of his life awake, telling more of his life stories to Ted, awaiting daylight, eager to continue living. It had not seemed to be his time to die. But it must have been, for he is gone.

Death is difficult for the one doing the dying *and* for the loved ones who remain. Questions are inevitable. No matter how a loved one dies, or where, or when, in addition to *how* and *why*, there is another recurring question: *What if* it had been different? *What if...?* For me, the question cast a recurring shadow that could not be ignored.

When the nagging question became too disturbing, I focused on it in an attempt to find the answer. I let myself imagine other scenarios in which his death might have occurred:

A traffic accident. He might have been a pedestrian or the occupant of a vehicle. What if *I* had been the one driving?

A stroke, followed by a long stay in a hospital or care center. Perhaps he could not speak or read or write, and then the loss of other abilities, and after an extended time, death.

A sudden, severe heart attack in his apartment, such that he could not get help due to his inability to grasp an emergency pull cord or to reach a phone. What if he had suffered many desperate hours, perhaps nearly a day, before dying alone?

I entertained other visions, all of them unpleasant and some far more upsetting. No matter what the circumstances surrounding the end of a life, it is possible to imagine a more grisly, untimely death. No longer did I wish my dad's death had been different.

I began to accept what was and to work on looking forward. In doing so I discovered renewed energy. It was as though one small phase of my grieving was complete.

Continuing the Quest

One evening on my way home from work, several days since my early morning visit to the park and its aged willow, I decided it was time to go again. I hoped doing so would salve my melancholy mood. After turning off the busy street, I drove under the graceful entrance arch and parked amongst a bevy of cars and SUVs. The play area was abuzz with the activity of families with children. The sounds were those of merriment and adventure; the atmosphere was joyful. If the *owl* was here, it was probably taking pleasure in the lighthearted fun.

Much as I appreciated the atmosphere of playful little ones exploring their world, I felt like an outsider. I was there for a purpose a world apart. I sensed at once that watching someone else's noisy fun would not be soothing to my distressed spirit...at least not today.

Noticing neither the raucous sentry crow nor the scampering squirrels, I chose to follow the path to my right that headed away from the playground. A gentle breeze carried the sweet fragrance of blossoms from the apple trees that waltzed their way around the perimeter of the pond at the end of the trail. A lone mallard drake near the far shore swam effortlessly on the water's mirror surface. I spied two bird nests...perhaps new, perhaps from last year. What appeared to be a yellow warbler flitted from tree to tree, never alighting long enough for me to know for sure. I stopped to bury my nose in a cluster of white blossoms and to fill my nostrils with the fragrance of spring. A small orange butterfly with dappled wings fluttered by. The reassuring elements of the spring scenario lightened my burden of grief.

I wandered back to the deck beside the willow tree, no longer noticing the sounds of the children. The sun, low in the west, shone welcomingly warm on my face. I remained there several minutes with my eyes closed, leaning against the railing, soaking up the warmth while birdsongs, echoing joyfully and insistently, urged me to take pleasure in them.

I returned to the parking area via a different trail. I noted a line of young conifers decorated with small cones on their highest branches. More evidence of new life. As I was ready to depart, I spied a multi-colored kite climbing the evening breeze, bringing memories of one specific morning's winds.

Tumbleweeds

I recalled my early morning drive to Nebraska on April 16th, the day of my dad's burial. Throughout the 230-mile trip to Wauneta, my vehicle was buffeted by wind gusts that must have reached fifty miles per hour. The voracious wind had an appetite for tumbleweeds, tumbleweeds that hurtled at me across the two-lane road ahead, approaching diagonally from the left. At times dozens of them blasted their way across the road. Eventually most became captured not by the wind that had expended so much energy pursuing them, but by a stationary barbed-wire fence.

I was fascinated by my reaction to the nearly gale-force wind. Typically, wind irritates and unnerves me. But that day, I welcomed its power. The strength of its energy filled me with courage. On a day involving the honoring of death, I sensed an aliveness that could not be denied.

With so many tumbleweeds careening toward my vehicle, it was inevitable at least one of them would collide with my car. It happened on three occasions. Each time, the result was the same:

the tumbleweed adhered to the grill of my car, intent on staying there for several miles.

I didn't mind a gigantic weed adorning the front of my car. But suppose I had viewed it philosophically as something I wanted to be rid of? Pushing against it would only result in it remaining where it was. The key to being *free of a tumbleweed* is not to push harder against it, but to release it by lessening the confrontation. Each time my vehicle captured a tumbleweed that day, I lifted my foot from the accelerator and it blew on by. This was one more insight resulting from my heightened awareness of the *now*.

The relentlessness of the powerful wind presented one more joyful experience on that momentous day. I witnessed tumbleweeds cavorting in dry cornfields. Perhaps they, too, were chasing wild horses and dancing with angels.

As for the owl, I hoped it was somewhere safe from the wind, perhaps in the shelter of a barn.

I spoke briefly at my dad's services. Everyone had experienced the intrusive wind, so I chose to incorporate it into my comments. I talked about its intrinsic strength. I reminded the small congregation of friends and relatives of the key role Dad had played in the development of shelterbelts throughout the state's formerly wide-open plains. These multi-row plantings of shrubs and trees, now mature, had been recommended to farmers for a trio of purposes: to slow wind erosion and loss of moisture in the soil, to buffer farmstead buildings from the prevailing north winds, and to provide critical shelter for wildlife. The day's intense winds served as a validation of the forethought of my dad and others in the early days of wildlife management.

The Poem

At his Nebraska funeral, as I had at the services at my dad's church a few days earlier, I spoke about his love of writing and of his fondness for a poem he had written several years earlier. He had read it for Mindy, Adam, and me when he was with us in May of 2001. When I spent time with him during his bout with pneumonia, he had expressed a desire to be able to share the poem with others. I took that as my cue. At both services, I read the poem he had written about spring:

When It's Spring
By Levi L. Mohler

When each crocus shows its head
You know it's spring.

When Emperor tulips show their red
You know it's spring.

When poplar catkins start to drop
And green grass makes robins hop,
When the finch's song won't stop
You know it's spring.

When the early robins sing
You know it's spring.

When warm sun bathes everything
You know it's spring.

When towhees start to scratch
In the leafy garden patch,
When days and nights no longer match
Then it's spring.

When the warblers have arrived
You know it's spring.

When the bees are all un-hived
You know it's spring.
When the earliest of flowers
Are anticipating showers,
When clouds build fluffy towers
Then it's spring.

It's really great to be alive
When it's spring.
Daybreak comes soon after five
When it's spring.

Other seasons of the year
Have their wonders, it is clear,
But nature's best is really here
When it's spring.

When I reached the phrase, "It's really great to be alive..." I was thankful my voice did not catch. At the close of each service, we presented each person with a daffodil-yellow bookmark with Dad's poem.

Letting Go

One evening in late April, I again was attempting to translate my internal struggles into words.

> What I am feeling tonight is akin to the desperation that swept over me late the day we buried Daddy. I am confronted with the jarring realization that the month Daddy died is nearly over. As long as the calendar displays the same now-familiar page, I am comforted by the proximity not only of his death, but also of the final few days of his life. It is my fear when the page turns the emotional distance will increase. Next month also contains the anniversary of the day I was born. Throughout the many years of my life, that day has been synonymous with joyful celebration. Two years ago my dad flew here for my birthday. That was the beginning of our unforgettable experience of living and traveling together

for seventeen days. This year the anticipation of my birthday is fraught with uncertainty.

It is not simply that time is passing or that my father has died. It's that everything is continuing to change. The process of change is an ongoing, never-ending mysterious truth. Change continues inside me: in my thoughts and perceptions. And it continues around me: in others, in world events, and in each bud that is unfolding further each of these warm spring days.

I keep reminding myself control lies in letting go. Things being released need not be big; I can start with smaller ones. Letting go of the need to have it still be this month vs. last month is one step. Letting go of the heavy-headed flowers in the funeral arrangements I brought home will be another. Letting go while continuing to love is like watching a toddler take uncertain steps alone, us no longer holding his hand for stability and security. Letting go allows new experiences. I must let go, knowing I need never let loose of the love.

Remnants

In the days that followed, I attempted to put into action the philosophy of letting go. About that experience, I wrote:

> It is a curious mix: some dried grasses, a couple of stems of soft grey pussy willows, a twisty branch, two stalks with purplish blossoms that remain intact close against their stems, some blue statice, and a few spires with fluffy goldenrod-like seedheads that show no signs of shedding. It is all I am able to salvage from the casket spray and numerous floral arrangements. I lovingly arrange them in the cut glass vase that had contained the vibrant bouquet sent by my friend Rebecca from California eleven days ago. Remnants...the lovely vase, the dried vegetation, a hint of color from the shriveled blossoms that refuse to drop their heads in mourning...remnants...expressions of loving remembrance.

As I emptied the balance of the contents into the wastebasket, a carpet of dried petals was laid upon my kitchen floor. I swept them together, ready to dispose of them, when I thought better of it. I sought out a small glass dish that had belonged to my dad's mother and scooped up the best of the potpourri of color, placing it into the cut-glass container. I pinched off a few tips of decorative ferns already in the trash and added them to the mix: more remnants to save awhile longer. The details of the shriveled forms were breathtaking, including purple larkspur such as my paternal grandmother grew in her garden, and wheat stalks, signifying the crops of the Great Plains...the land into which my father had been born and into which his body has been returned.

Remnant...that which remains. Am I, too, a remnant? Am I something that has survived, mirroring my dad in whatever ways I can? How does what physically remains relate to the loved one who is gone? Do remnants matter? Is it OK to want to have something to see and to touch that was his or that reminds me of him, or should memories suffice? Is it all right not to let go of the flowers and petal potpourri...yet? I have much to learn about letting go.

"Everything in its time," I hear myself answer. When the stalks of dried flowers and pussy willows collect dust and spiderwebs, they may seem less wonderful. When the bowl holding the dried petals is needed for jelly for a family meal, the contents can be relinquished. But for now, these remnants are gentle reminders of my dad.

And there are others: on the hook in the bathroom, the robe he used when he came to visit; on my mantel, the photograph of him and my daughter Mindy on her wedding day, the two of them radiating happiness. There's the tiny stand-up mirror he gave to Mom even before they were engaged. He wanted me to have it after she died. The slim, gold-toned frame is delicately engraved. On the reverse, along with a poem, is a picture of two graceful swans and a lady in a full-skirted long dress holding a fan. The poem reads:

My Sweetheart

I thought that you would like to know
That someone's thoughts go where you go;
That someone never can forget
The hours we spent since first we met;
That life is richer, sweeter far
For such a sweetheart as you are;
And now my constant prayer will be
That God may keep you safe for me!

We called it "the sweetheart mirror." It was one of Mom's most beloved treasures, kept safely away from everyday life in the center drawer of her dresser. I, too, treasure it and wonder where I eventually might keep it. Its words convey hope, as though I, too, am to be "kept safe."

Remembrance

Beyond experiencing grief and learning its life-evolving lessons lay relief in the joy and honor I discovered in remembrance. One day in late April, I received an exquisite sympathy card. Its graceful calligraphy conveyed serenity, and its black, red, and rich gold leaf imparted a quiet strength. The calligraphed character, the Chinese symbol for *remembrance*, offered a comforting message. Remembrance was a holy experience, growing out of the dust and tears of grief.

I had gone *in search of the owl*. *Remembrance* was the blessed word for which I had been searching. *Remembrance* was like unlocking part of the mystery. The essence of that word freed me to honor and to rejoice. Remembrance encouraged me to reflect on all my father symbolized, all he loved, all he was to me, all he had shared with the world, and more. Out of the noun *remembrance* comes *the act of remembering.* The word *remembrance* carries a sacred, solemn tone; in contrast, *remembering* indicates action and aliveness, an ongoing activity that weaves itself amongst the threads of daily life. Remembering is effortless and spontaneous. Its surprise appearance is welcome when some aspect of an experience, person, or thing brings thoughts of my dear dad.

My life will be filled with memories of my dad, be they drawn-out or brief. I can reflect intentionally when I need him with me and I can take pleasure in the spontaneity of his company at unexpected times. Whether in the form of tears, smiles, or profound thankfulness, *remembering* will present me with endless gifts.

A Native American Belief

A belief common among Native Americans is that one dies only when one is no longer remembered...when no person, thing, or idea on which the individual had any effect can be found. My father, then, may live forever.

He was a teacher, a coach, a writer, a published author, a parent, a grandfather, and an environmentalist. He planted and tended lilacs and trees and rosebushes that are still growing, producing glorious blossoms that bring joy to all who see them. He encouraged young people to follow their dreams, creating in them substantive values that may be passed on forever. He smiled at everyone and modeled a curious, pleasant demeanor. His strength of character and love of life, like seeds, will continue to grow. Nebraska shelterbelts are living monuments to his foresight and dedication to the environment. Concepts he developed in wildlife management continue to be built on today. Through the Nature Conservancy, he helped to protect and preserve wild lands far into the future.

Ripples created by his existence will extend around the globe and come back upon themselves, criss-crossing in an endless interwoven web. Yes, his living on this earth made a difference.

Telling the Story

Telling the story...his story...my story. Time and time again, it unfolds. "How is your dad?" someone asks. My heart skips a beat. "My dad died," I say. I don't know if the words are more difficult for me to say or for *the someone* to hear. I take a deeper-than-usual breath before telling the story one more time.

For all who have lost a loved one, it is the same: the need to tell the story...to experience one more time the reality of what happened. It becomes a ritual; telling the story is a mantra, its familiar words offering a degree of comfort. Each time I listen to my explanation of the *how* of it...his death...I am listening for the *why* of it as well. With each telling a new wrinkle in the mystery smoothes out.

Over and over and over it is told: the story, couched in terms of my limited understanding of death and loss. Am I telling the story for me or for the listener? Am I telling it out of respect for my dad? Sometimes those who have heard it before are also listening; am I telling it to make it deeply embedded in them, so it becomes their story as well? One they, too, will tell? Time and time again, for days...weeks now, I've been the storyteller for all who will listen. For the rest of my life, and longer I hope, the story of my dear dad will be told.

Sometimes, through some serendipitous connection with a stranger, I begin the story again; for them, a shorter version. The stranger becomes close, respectful, honoring my need to share my experience, my loss, and my understanding of what has happened, or lack thereof. No one has ever said, in words or in stance, "I don't have time to listen to your story." They listen; a few give their own version of sympathy or reassurance. Sometimes it's not the best match for what I want or need, but I know they mean well.

Telling the story helps me. However, most days, I also deal with rapid, disconcerting emotional changes. The roller coaster called grieving lifts me and hurtles me down all too far, all too fast, time after time after time. At ten thirty one night I wrote:

> I am looking forward to falling asleep tonight. One of the blessings of sleep is one cannot sob and sleep at the same time. I've been crying for almost two hours...wailing, sobbing, sometimes moaning, and calling out for my dad.
>
> Out of desperation I phoned my daughter, then a couple of friends. They each listened. They were concerned. But no one can help. Grieving is lonely stuff. You must do it all by yourself. You do it in a fog, or in darkness. No, it's worse. It's in the absolute absence of light.
>
> It's nighttime. Again, it's a Sunday evening, when Daddy often would call after a stint of jigsaw puzzle work. The phone would ring; at the other end of the line I'd hear his always cheerful, "Hello, Jean, this is your dad." Never again. Never again. I simply need to sleep.

Bird Dream

The following evening I wrote:

> In my dream last night, I was in an unfamiliar wooded area watching birds. After observing several common species, I noted with amusement a large bird reclining on a fat branch. In a casual pose, with its head propped against the trunk of the tree and its feathers fluffed out, it appeared to be basking in the sun. Although I had never seen one relaxing on its back, there it was: the bird was an owl.
>
> After I awoke this morning, I attempted to analyze the curious dream. My effortless discovery of the owl had been in tune with its informal posture and cartoonish character. The owl's blissful contentment and lighthearted pose differed markedly from the upright stance and wise, stern countenance of the traditional representation of an owl. Was the dream

telling me to take life less seriously? Which owl held answers to my quest...the one in my dream, or the solemn owl? Was wisdom to be discovered in both? Maybe I didn't need to choose. Perhaps they were just different facets of the same being.

Spending My Inheritance

Eventually the issue of Dad's inheritance demanded attention. Equating my dad's death with a financial benefit brought to mind the phrase *cold cash*. I shuddered; the indifference of those words was inconsistent with the powerful emotions of my loss. I struggled with the concept of my father's death creating something I didn't have before. At first I gave it minimal thought, but when I received paperwork in the mail needing my signature, I could no longer ignore this aspect of death.

My father had been a teacher and later a state employee, never earning more than a modest salary. However, what became impressive was the care he had taken over the years to avoid being a financial burden to anyone and to provide a financial inheritance for his three children. The value in dollars of what we were to receive was relatively small; however, given his advanced age and level of income throughout his working years, it was remarkable that a man not trained in financial matters had managed so wisely what assets he did have. He and Mother had lived well within their means. Daddy had remained in good health until the end. The result was rather than debts, he had left us a cushion of financial comfort.

Some of my financial gift would be translated into a memorial to my dad; most would be added to my nest egg. Perhaps each year I would buy a small birthday gift for myself and consider it from him. A portion of the money would go toward paying off a couple of burdensome debts that, while not large, were making my life uncomfortable. I felt guilty spending the funds my dad had worked so hard to save. However, a dear friend pointed out he would have wanted me to use it for things that would bring comfort or pleasure to my life; I need not save it all. I laughed when I considered the idea of using some of the money to install an owl perch, high in the gable of my house.

I'd been *spending my inheritance* all my life. This soon-to-be-acquired financial bequest would be inconsequential when compared to the worth of what I had inherited in another fashion. I had learned from my father's strong values, his positive attitude, his appreciation of life and respect for all its forms, and his expressions of love. I hope my demeanor, my outlook, and my interaction with others echo my dad's qualities. *Spending my inheritance* took on new meaning for me. I will happily dole out a penny of a precious perception, a quarter in the form of a compliment, or a dollar of a delightful discovery. I intend to share that part of my inheritance every day.

Like My Dad

An acquaintance I had not seen since my dad died crossed the room to give me a hug and to whisper she was sorry about my dad. I don't know her well but am always glad to be around her. She exudes wonderfully loving, positive energy. After reading his obituary, she commented about what an interesting life he had led. She winked at me and said, "Sounds like Jean."

If my life bore some resemblance to my dad's life, I felt thankful and pleased. I guessed it was all part of *the inheritance*.

Thankful for Life

"I am thankful for life." That simple and profound statement prefaced my dad's remarks at Thanksgiving dinner nearly five months before his death. As many families do on that holiday, those of us gathered at my daughter and son-in-law's table were sharing what we were thankful for that year. His succinct words, although so typical of him, still amazed me. He did not say, "I am thankful to be alive." Rather, he spoke of the all-inclusive concept of *life*. When all is said and done, life is at the core of all we value. For without life, there is no love, no experience of health, happiness, or success, no relationships to cherish, no trees nor birds nor flowers, and no next generation.

"I am thankful for life." He stated it perfectly. Was he more aware of his mortality than we realized or was he simply celebrating a truth he held dear?

I, too, am thankful for life. This experience with death has reminded me death is intrinsically partnered with life. For all life eventually ends in death.

One Month

Once again, it seemed too soon. I wasn't ready but the day arrived anyway. It was one month since my father had died. That evening I wrote:

> This has been a challenging day. I struggled to get out of bed. My stomach was bloated. Before departing I ate a small breakfast; coffee didn't have its usual appeal. Tired and despondent, everything I attempted happened in slow motion. For the first few hours at work, I buried myself in mundane tasks. My customary outgoing demeanor and eagerness to interact with co-workers and customers were lacking. I plodded through the day.
>
> This evening I talked nearly an hour with my sister by phone. Her voice was monotone and listless. She had not been able to sleep until after daybreak this morning. Her appetite was waning also. As though to solidify them in our memories, we walked

ourselves through various events, including the day of Daddy's near-death heart attack.

The longer I go without talking to Daddy, the harder it is for me. I find myself storing away little stories or observations to share with him. Sometimes it's a question I want to ask him, something about Mom's illness or about his parents, which only he would know. The realization I can never ask, and he can never answer, leaves me numb.

Generation Gap

Soon after, I wrote about my disconcerting perception of the term *generation gap*.

> I see it not as a gap but rather a deep, bottomless chasm. I stand at the edge, dizzy, tears streaming down my face, my sobs becoming echoes of melancholy sadness. Somewhere into the abyss my mother and father have disappeared. My generation stands not proudly at the forefront, but precariously on the brink. Ahead of us: no one.
>
> I am no one's daughter, no one's little girl. My siblings and I are the generation at the edge of the crevasse. I shudder, almost wanting to fall and to disappear into oblivion, for now that I have no parents, I am an orphan. I long to hold my own daughter in my arms. Even more I long to have her hold me.

Then I take a mental step backward. What I am remembering steadies me, giving me reassurance.

One generation is gone. However, before the sun set on my parents' generation, a shadow was cast behind me, behind my daughter, demarcating yet another. My first grandchild, a boy, is to be born this summer.

Birthday Eve

On the eve of my birthday I sat at my antique library table writing. I composed a short letter to Mindy to include in a belated sympathy card. The card read, "In Sympathy at the Loss of Your Grandfather." Offering compassion to someone else, acknowledging her loss, felt good. The text of the letter was as follows:

My Dearest Mindy,

What a bittersweet time this is. Your first child, your son, is growing within you, even as you are without your Grandpa Mohler. He loved you so much, Mindy. He was proud of your goals and the strong, beautiful woman you had become. He loved your spirit.

I took pleasure from the strong bond that was developing between you two: your shared love of journaling, tending roses, watching birds, and the lov-

ing letters you exchanged. How grateful I am now to see aspects of him in you. In you, he is still alive.

How prophetic of you to know to send the little paper-maché chickadee to be with him in his final days. He may have heard its call, as he left us.

I know we share sadness he never had the chance to see your infant son. I know he and you would have loved that opportunity. But something tells me he is watching out for us as we continue our lives.

Treasure your joy. It is what your grandpa would have wanted.

I love you.

Mom

Even though she and her husband did not live far from me, I wanted to mail the card and note to her. I planned to do so the following day.

There was an incongruity in celebrating my birthday when the two people who had given me life were dead. I didn't know what to anticipate, but trusted the owl would guide me through my day.

Earlier in the evening my neighbor had presented me with a small paper bag, stapled shut. She prompted me to read her handwritten message on the outside. It promised she'd be thinking of me "on my special day." She always remembered my birthday because it was the same as her daughter's. Smiling mischievously, she had said, "Someone told me to get this for you. It was your dad. He called me."

I guess anything is possible. As curious as I was about the contents, I made myself wait to open the unexpected package.

My Birthday

I arose early. I pampered myself with a luxurious bath followed by a different-for-me breakfast of orange juice, scrambled eggs, and fried potatoes. Between bites, I opened one birthday card, planning to save the others for later. Curious about my neighbor's gift, I opened it next. It was tiny…it was glass…and, most fittingly, it was a magically whimsical bird.

I didn't need to be at work until ten, so I had time for some early morning errands: the first, to a nearby store to purchase a flowering hanging basket for my patio…a birthday gift to myself. I returned home to hang it. The cascading purple verbena looked especially joyful in contrast to my otherwise neglected patio.

I had received a coupon from a card shop for a discount on an item of my choice. It was valid all month, but using it on my special day would make it more fun. So I drove to the shop near my workplace. It opened at nine, allowing ample time to browse.

I selected a slim black journal with gilt-edged leaves. I intended to resume regular diary-keeping, following my dad's lead. For my final treat I bought a flavored coffee I could savor as I started my workday.

It was a pleasant day. Fun was interspersed with business. I received many thoughtful greetings from friends and family. My most unexpected gift, a box of four chocolate truffles, was from the mail carrier at work.

Adam was out of town; therefore, Mindy and I celebrated by dining at a restaurant with fondue-everything. Swiss cheese. Steak. Shrimp. Fruit. And fabulous dark *and* white chocolate fondues for dessert. With no one waiting for us to get home, we took our time, lingering over each bite and savoring our girl time. Part of our conversation revolved around her baby. We were excitedly anticipating having him in our midst.

My day was almost over. It had indeed been special…overflowing with people and experiences I enjoyed. I was almost asleep, cozy in the comfort of new memories, when I became aware of the void: for the first time in my life, I had not talked to my dad on my birthday.

Die Young

"Those who love deeply never grow old; they may die of old age, but they die young." So read a quotation from an inspirational book my dad had owned. Playwright Sir Arthur Wing Pinero could have been writing about my father. My dad loved deeply and well. All who knew him were aware of his devotion to our mom, his wife Luella. They had been married sixty-seven years when she died. Daddy told people the key to his great life was choosing the right partner. When Mom was still alive but in the advanced stages of dementia, he said, "Your mother, I can't praise her enough. She is perfect for me. I love her so much." Those words made a lasting impression on me.

Daddy adopted a goal in keeping with Sir Arthur's quote. My dad wanted "to die young, at an old age." And he achieved that goal. There was nothing old about him except his body. He loved meeting people, going places, learning new things. He loved, as he called it, *adventuring*. My father also loved words, but I believe *boredom* was not in his vocabulary.

My father's life was filled with many familiar routines, but compared to many seniors, his acceptance of change was remarkable. An excellent example is from the final week of his life. At the retirement center, he had been accustomed to staying up until eleven at night and rising about eight thirty. But in the hospital, medical procedures and doctors' visits began early, usually with hospital staff waking him to record his vital signs; his breakfast arrived before eight o'clock. Rather than becoming frustrated, he said, "I'm glad I'm getting onto an earlier schedule with my daily activities." Yes, my father was an amazing man.

A Surprise Visitor

It was the tenth of May. A late spring snowstorm had swept in overnight, creating havoc. I had been awakened at 4:45 by a branch falling onto the roof. I was thankful I had believed the weather forecast and transferred my hanging basket to the garage. At dawn I viewed the chaos caused by the too-heavy burden of wet snow: broken trees, tender new leaves mixed into the snow, and delicate underdeveloped seeds from the red maple tree, distributed too soon. Rather than a pristine snow, this one was ugly, littered with debris…an unfortunate collision of winter and spring. Now and then I heard muted hammerings as clumps of snow became dislodged from sagging branches to percussion their presence upon my roof.

My daughter called a little before nine thirty to discuss plans for Mother's Day. As we conversed, I gazed through the double doors to the patio covered with four inches of wet snow. Protruding from the edges of snow-disguised clay pots, the new growth of perennials lay awkwardly splayed. Crushed. The locust branches with their half-sprouted leaves hung low over the round wrought iron table, itself bearing a circular cap of the snow-and-leaf mix. The clouded sky was nondescript. The entire view was soggy, burdened, and grey.

Suddenly I said, "I can't believe it!" A brilliant western tanager had landed on the lowest-hanging branch of the locust tree. Our conversation nearly stopped for almost a minute as the flashy red-and-yellow-feathered creature stayed there, turning after several seconds in one position, as if to demonstrate the full array of its splendor. As quickly as it appeared, it flitted out of sight.

The male western tanager is one of the most colorful wild birds in the continental United States. It had been featured for decades on the cover of Roger Tory Peterson's *Field Guide to Western Birds* and on a United States postage stamp celebrating the art of John James Audubon. Bird-lover that I am, during the thirty-five years I'd lived in Colorado, I had never seen one.

I'd been in search of the owl, not a western tanager. However, its appearance on this dreary morning while I was talking with my daughter was wondrously serendipitous. Had this winged angel, in the form of a bird, been my dad's doing? Was this his way of being in touch?

Roots

I believe as each of our lives unfolds, a unique patchwork quilt of personal experiences is created. The next piece to be added to mine, outlined with featherstitches like those my grandmother favored, promised to be soft, significant, and comforting.

The presence of my father's family on this continent pre-dates the Revolutionary War. I belong to generation nine. My roots can be traced to the 1730s in what is now eastern Pennsylvania. Quite coincidently, I flew there in mid-May to attend job-related workshops in the village where my paternal grandfather was born in the late 1800s.

The rural area was moist and lush and beautifully green. Planting of crops was underway in the rolling fields; grass was luxuriantly thick. Acknowledging my loss, the lovely bleeding hearts were blooming. My time there was one of gentle greys, mist, and frequent drizzle. The weather created an environment for reflection. However, only after the workshops ended could my reflection and exploration begin. A day and a half remained before I would depart for home.

The farmstead where my dad's family settled still exists. Thanks to a buffer of woods and grassland, its rural nature has been preserved. The substantial house, constructed of native stone, has been well maintained. I had been there five years earlier; I was comfortable knocking on the side door that opened to the kitchen and the primary living area of the home. The owner responded, remembered me, and gave her blessing to my request to photograph the grounds and exterior of her house. (*Her* house? To me, it would forever be *our* house...the *Mohler* house.)

I was thankful for the opportunity to be on the land my family had trod centuries ago. Although the earth and ancient trees were wet, for now, it had stopped raining. I extended the legs of my tripod and secured my camera body to its top. Through the lens, I composed an image. I was about to click the shutter when an Eastern bluebird flew over my shoulder and into view through my camera lens. The bright male landed on a fencepost between me and the house. Comfortable with my presence, he stayed put as I inched forward with my photographic equipment between exposures. I had a new roll of film in my camera, so I was able to snap several pictures before he winged away.

As I was preparing to stow my camera and tripod in the trunk of my rental car, two birds provided another unexpected experience. A pair of mallard ducks flew into view, barely airborne, from behind the house. They rose in unison and flew clockwise...beyond where I was standing. I pivoted with my back to the house, my neck craned, to watch their circular flight. They disappeared behind the left side of the house, connecting their circle to its starting point. It was a curiously short flight for two ducks. The house, symbolic of my roots, had been at the center of their flight; the flight had included me in the circle.

I recalled the circular flight of the crow in the park a few weeks earlier. He also had drawn a clockwise circle. "Do birds always travel clockwise as they circle in flight?" I needed to find out.

Owl Pellets

The morning after I returned from Pennsylvania, I recorded the following unpleasant thoughts.

> Owl pellets...bird poop...leavings...only these am I finding today. Back home from my trip. Feeling angry, frustrated, exhausted. My house, a place of cluttered chaos. Outside, broken trees evidence their mutilation by the storm ten days ago.
>
> Life has been so difficult since my dad died. This morning I am overwhelmed, panic-stricken, as I was early on. I wish I would cry. I am disgusted with myself. And I am angry he is gone.

Truth and Beauty

I could have been looking in a mirror: the female face appeared disbelieving and sad. Tears filled her eyes. She had just learned of my dad's death. I knew Gail as a casual business acquaintance. She had met him only once. Yet she felt connected enough with my dad's authentic nature that his death became her loss. As I watched her eyes and the slouched dejection in her body language, I saw myself. I saw how alike we were, we who knew little about each other.

Her sadness also conveyed a truth. The truth was about the ability of genuineness to create connections where none before existed.

A core value of my father's was honesty, expressed via his down-to-earth interactions with others. He lived out his many years enjoying the true beauty he discovered in everything…and in everyone. My father was an emotional man who was easily moved. A simple memory could move him to tears. Yet my father also was incredibly stable, solid in his sense of self. He was optimistic, clear in his purpose, and true to himself. His truth and beauty radiated. Thus he had become connected with the woman who tearfully expressed her condolences. His genuineness I saw in her. I understood one more aspect of the multi-faceted concept of life and death.

Timetable for the Search

How long would my *search for the owl* continue? The emotional nature of the time following my father's death made me sensitive to my own being in ways I had never experienced. *Life*, which I used to think I had figured out, had shuttled me down a detour with unfamiliar turns and vistas. It was a long detour. After a few months, I began to understand this detour *was* my new life. I would never get back to the familiar road I had known so well.

And how long would I be consumed by *grief*? At first, without admitting it, part of me had been expecting to get through the process and continue somewhat as before. But the process of grieving together with the void created by death had made me look at things anew. A friend asked if I assumed by a certain time that I would be done mourning. I knew she meant I would *not* be. By then I had figured that out. I could determine neither the timeline nor the intensity of the process. Other than my attitude there was little I could control.

Perhaps the timelines for grieving and for the *search for the owl* were different. Perhaps they would parallel for a while, later to diverge. Some aspects of grieving would continue indefinitely; however, the same might be true of my quest for revelations about the mystery of life and death. Perhaps the two were so intertwined they had become one. One thing was certain: I was encountering more questions than answers.

Springtime Forgotten

Spring was abloom when my father entered the hospital: vibrant tulips and the brilliant yellows of daffodils and forsythia had punctuated the soft greens. After his death, spring became foggy—not literally, but in my mind. Days passed and I had no idea where they went. By mid-May, well past time to plant the season's annuals, my patio garden remained bare except for my hanging basket and the welcome foliage of potted perennials that had survived the late snow.

For me, the essence of springtime was nearly forgotten...lost amongst the multitude of changes that buffeted my being and clouded my vision. Some days I managed to bend, adjust, and refocus. Often death had me in its shadow. Sometimes I thought the sun would come out and death's shadow, ironically, would disappear. There were moments I forgot my dad had died. Most days...I cried. A little plateau along this steep road, a little respite from grief, would have been welcome.

And what of my *search for the owl*? Was it also forgotten? Was the search still on?

A Place for Watching

One weekend I appreciated a welcome escape from the neglect of my home. On Saturday evening and Sunday morning, I wrote about the agreeable environment I discovered.

> I am dog sitting at my daughter and son-in-law's tonight while they are out of town. Standing at the kitchen sink, I look out across the broad sweep of back lawn to the tall maple tree with its stout trunk and thick branches bearing new leaves. I take in the spirea and lilacs laden with blossoms and the sheltering trees beyond the fence line. I am buoyed by my visual tour of the yard. Here, springtime has been neither lost nor forgotten.
>
> My gaze lights on the window ledge. A small pair of binoculars lies atop my daughter's bird identification book. The book, a gift to her from my father and mother when she was eight years old, contains handwritten notes from her grandfather about

birds she likely would see in her backyard. The comfortable continuity of generations is epitomized in these simple physical items, kept where she can, as he did, use them to enjoy the winged creatures that frequent the environment called home.

It is now Sunday morning. My granddog Jake is stretched out in the sun. For me, the covered patio provides a welcome retreat for writing. I watch a drab female sparrow tending a nest in a simple wooden birdhouse hanging fifteen feet from where I sit. Flapping noisily, a raucous speckled starling attempts to gain a foothold on the suet cage. An orange-headed house finch lands on the cylindrical feeder suspended from a low branch of the maple and feeds watchfully. A graceful concrete birdbath in the far corner of the garden awaits visitors. A plump robin does battle with an earthworm in the lawn: the robin wins. Two frisky squirrels play tag around the trunk of the maple tree. Another bold squirrel tiptoes along the fence-top, daring to trespass into Jake's domain. Quick to spot it, Jake emphatically chases the trespasser away. Bird songs are the morning's music.

My dad visited here on more than one occasion. Twice he spent the day while I was at work. This oasis must have reminded him of the backyard he loved so much...the yard at the place he called home from 1954 until 1998. A large silver maple, older but similar in shape and growth habit to this one, was positioned in the left half of his lawn. Lilacs, as they did here, provided a backdrop for the yard. Spires of lavender phlox, a favorite of swallowtail butterflies, thrived adjacent to his patio as they do near my daughter's. In each yard stood a birdbath, a prominent feature providing a setting for frequent surprises. Mature trees in surrounding neighborhoods offered a natural habitat for urban wildlife. The two places were in synchrony. No wonder I sense harmony here.

The search for the owl brought me here, to sense the continuity of values and glimpse another slice of nature. The burgeoning habitat, the urban wildlife, and the pleasure my daughter finds in them have evolved as a matter of course.

As I am about to stop writing, a mourning dove flies past and away...as if, at least for now, to withdraw mourning from my experience.

Tiring and Challenging

Eventually, six weeks had passed since the burial. The days preceding those events, laden with phone calls, difficult decisions, and travel, had been *long and tiring and challenging*.

After these six weeks, again my days were *long and tiring and challenging*. I was still grieving; sadness engulfed the depths of my being. Almost without fail, someone appeared daily in the ordinary business of living to share a story of loss and to listen to at least a bit of mine. The need to tell the story of my dad's sudden illness and death remained strong. With each telling it became a bit more real. One day a customer explained that her own eighty-some-year-old mother was in the hospital with pneumonia. Pneumonia: too often a kiss of death for the aged. I listened carefully, sparing her my story.

Six weeks earlier, I had been tired because of crying, played-out emotions, and sleep deprivation. Now much of my tiredness resulted from efforts to confront numerous long-neglected tasks. Life was challenging in a different way. With the novelty of death gone, the energy I found earlier in accepting life's changes was waning. It was difficult for me to appreciate the many positive qualities of life that remained. I wanted to call time out.

I couldn't, so I did what I could. I ate sensibly and fulfilled my job responsibilities. I attempted to accomplish something extra each day and to sleep eight hours each night. And I wrote:

> As I write, I gain increased awareness of my feelings, my transformation, and something churning in the hidden depths of my knowingness. At times, aspects of it escape, sometimes joyfully, sometimes with gut-wrenching pain. The essence of my grieving process is here, in the words foot-printing their way across these pages. Tonight, I feel tired and insignificant. My words appear thin and brittle, leaving only puny prints upon the page.
>
> Somewhere the owl must be watching for me. I must continue to believe all is well.

Soapweed

I was relieved when I noticed the cream-colored, bell-shaped flowers of yucca plants beginning to open, a gift bestowed by my father's favorite season. They adorned the tall stalks rising from the whorl of the yuccas' spiked leaves. Nicknamed "soapweed" because of the detergent properties of its roots, this plant grows profusely in the dry plains of western Nebraska where my father lived as a boy. Just as bold-colored hollyhocks conjure up pleasant memories of my youth, picturesque yucca blossoms struck a familiar chord for my dad, resonating with the attributes of familiarity and predictability he associated with *home*.

Several years after moving from Pennsylvania to Nebraska, my grandfather had established a homestead near Wauneta. It was there, in a sod house, my dad was born.

Four years ago this month, my father and I, on one of our famous adventures, drove to western Nebraska. Our goal had been to reach the site of that homestead and sod house. The land was now interior to a cattle ranch, a more fitting use for it than the dryland crop farm which had been such a challenge to my dad's parents.

We were granted permission to "trespass." Although he had not set foot on the site for more than fifty years, Dad knew intuitively how to get there. Following his directions, I turned off the dusty county road and maneuvered the rutted pasture trail nearly a mile. We passed through two barbed-wire gates, being careful to close each one behind us. Buffalo grass was the predominant ground cover in this part of the Sand Hills. Once out of the car, as he had done many times before, my dad leaned down, this time steadying himself with his cane, to examine the familiar grass's growth habit and to call my attention to it, the grass that had grown beneath his feet throughout his early years. Again I observed its short, coarse, grey-green nature and flag-like seed heads.

The sod home of his childhood had long since returned to nature. However, near where it had been, the windmill constructed by my grandfather towered above the landscape. At the base of a small hill, we examined the concrete cistern, nearly one hundred years old. He pointed to a far hillside. He recalled his mother saying, "I spy the thimble," when she had discovered a newborn calf there…a calf forever known as *Thimble*. He showed me the location overlooking a shallow ravine where he often sprawled on his stomach as a lad, waiting for his older brother and half-sisters on their way home from the nearby country school. I saw the site of his mom's garden, where she had shown him the small nest in the bean plant. He overflowed with stories that day and I, the eager listener, was spellbound with the new revelations.

Our afternoon visit had seemed timeless and magical: the sky, an uninterrupted blue; the temperature, neither hot nor cold. Meadowlarks sang their joyful songs for us. And scattered across the hillsides were picturesque yuccas with their showy flowers.

It was that time of year again. A few hardy yuccas in untamed areas near my home were again in bloom. Their stately display brought welcome recollections of my roots. I knew each year at yucca-blossom time, I would relive the homestead visit with my dad.

Winds of Change

The joy I found in seeing the yucca blossoms was short-lived. My early June writing reflected new challenges.

> In places where strong prevailing winds blow consistently from one direction, trees grow accordingly: not upright but leaning, sculpted and groomed by the incessant winds. Although I try to remain vertical, I am buffeted by the harsh winds of change. Unlike prevailing winds, these are more fickle, assuming a new direction at will. Just as I have leaned into one challenge, the wind reverses and I nearly fall flat on my face. It is disconcerting. There is no way to prepare against the next onslaught other than to assume a wide stance.
>
> I have become accustomed to analyzing the changes within me with regard to my dad's death. Now an emotional gust from another direction nearly

toppled me. This was a get-together at the home of my ex-husband and his wife in honor of my expectant daughter and son-in-law. Most of the guests were people with whom I've had minimal contact since my divorce. I've been single for eighteen years and have changed a lot in that time, becoming more independent and involved with photography and politics. Trying to interact with them as who I have become, while they could relate to me only as who I had been, was a challenge. Seeing the transformation of the house my ex-husband and I had built also felt uncomfortable. In many ways the energy there was disorienting.

Emotionally drained, I returned to the comforting familiarity of my home. I longed to talk to my loving father, who had told me often how proud he was of my values and the choices I made in life. In the hours and days that followed, the return to my friends and familiar activities soothed my shaken spirit.

Time

But the roller coaster of emotions continued. Mourning shrouded my existence. More grieving necessitated more writing.

> We humans have long had a fascination with time. Writers have chosen the subject repeatedly, creating pieces that are poetic, philosophical, spiritual, metaphysical, or simply prosaic. Moral maxims chasten us about wasting time and encourage us to use it wisely and to spend it well.
>
> The grieving process, however, sets time aside. Time makes no sense at all to one who grieves. We who mourn take time in ways we otherwise wouldn't, feeling justified for letting time pass without routine tasks being accomplished. For now, grief is a thin curtain separating me from the concept of time. I often find myself not caring how long I cry or how long I write. No measure of time

can delineate my sadness. Neither can my preoccupation with the search for the owl be confined by an element called time.

What a cruel juxtaposition, when I enter a time-sensitive space: an appointment, the need to arrive at work on time, or an interaction with a clock-watcher. I question the compartmentalization of time in this experience we call Western civilization. I visualize the Native Americans utilizing the sun and moon to shape their activities. That approach feels more compatible with my grief than does the counting of minutes and hours.

I am thankful for the luxury of being able to grieve; it is important work, it takes time…is deserving of my time. It is imperative I feel the feelings that cut to my core and make me so genuinely human.

I am thankful also for the time I take to write.

Anger

At times I felt…and wrote…only *anger*.

> Damn it! I want my dad back! I get angry when people try to console me about my loss with the reminder that soon I will have a new grandson, inferring my grandson can replace my father. Tonight I am angry…angry my dad had to die, angry I am so alone. I have cried a long time tonight. It is now two months since my dad died. Yes, he died. I hate the terms made his transition, passed away, left this plane of existence. Damn it…he died! I hate it. I hurt. I miss him. I don't give a #*!% about anything. I cried myself to sleep last night. I guess I'll do the same tonight.
>
> I'm struggling to accomplish some important tasks. I want to sew a kimono sleeper for my little grandson similar to the one I made for my daughter

before she was born. Soon I'll be out of town to deal with Mom and Dad's belongings. I don't know how I can do it all. Mindy asked if I can plant the annuals in her yard: an impossible task for her because of her protruding belly. I'm looking forward to doing the planting and the sewing but I don't know when there will be time.

I feel overwhelmed. I am exhausted from crying. And I am too angry and too sad and too tired to write about the owl...

PART TWO

A Surreal Summer

Every Step of the Journey

A Zen parable says, "Every step of the journey *is* the journey." The next step in my *search for the owl* involved another long drive; at its end, the city my mom and dad called home for nearly fifty years.

My sister, brother, and I had carved five days out of our schedules to meet in Boise. We would make decisions about the dispersal of the last of Mom and Dad's belongings, including the contents of Daddy's apartment and multiple storage units. It promised to be a Herculean task.

The eve of my departure, I spent some time with my *soon-to-be-a-mom* daughter on her backyard patio. As we conversed, a red-winged blackbird visited the bird feeder. She remarked that it was the first one she'd seen there. I remembered that bird being the most common species seen on car trips with Daddy. Another curious coincidence. I'd be watching for them tomorrow.

When it was time for me to go, we hugged. I urged her to take care of herself. In turn, she urged me to drive safely. I fervently hoped I would be back before my grandson was born.

Nearly two years of record-breaking drought had ravaged Colorado and Wyoming. The wet spring, therefore, was cause for rejoicing. I witnessed the bluegrass lawns in the city resurrecting from their brownness, but had not seen the countryside for several weeks. The hills and mountain slopes were a rich green. As I drove into southeastern Wyoming's majestic high plains, the deep colors of the wild grasses and undergrowth hardly looked real. I watched for antelope. Against the intense hues the light-colored antelope no longer were camouflaged, but contrasted markedly to their verdant environment.

The cloud-laden June sky enhanced the dramatic vistas. Grey gossamer streamers of virga hung from the distant clouds in ever-changing patterns. High amongst them, lightning frolicked. I was on an adventure with an ever-changing backdrop.

Suddenly, one hundred yards ahead, I saw it: shiny, reflective pavement and a curtain of water. Within seconds, it was like driving into a waterfall. I switched on the windshield wipers, and seconds later, turned them to high. They were no match for the torrents of rain. I witnessed the rapid flashes of lightning but I could barely hear the thunder beyond the deafening noise of the rain. The vehicle ahead of me suddenly slipped sideways out of its lane. A fraction of a second later, the same thing happened to mine. Hydroplaning. As I lifted my foot from the accelerator, I heard Daddy's question, "Do you have good tires on your car?" All of this happened nearly simultaneously. And yes, with good tires, good luck, or whatever, both vehicles proceeded without further incident.

I was experiencing sensory overload: the lightning, the racket of the rain and thunder, the feeling of the smooth leather of the steering wheel I had been gripping so tightly, and the immersion in the smell of moist sage. The rain lessened. It was as if I had entered a perfumery and the specialty of the day was sage. It was intoxicating and wondrous.

Within minutes and a matter of miles, the rain subsided. The air was pristine; it seemed as though I could see forever. Nudged at either side by gently rolling mountains, the wide floor of the plains was strewn with color. A peaceful meadow beside a meandering stream was showing its wild side with a riot of yellow blossoms. Elsewhere, rafts of blue decorated the hillsides. A dramatic big-screen movie, except better. This was the real thing.

I noted the highway marker. Eight miles ahead was the town where I had seen the second owl two months before. Should I stop there again? Absolutely!

The sign at the edge of town read, "Population 433." Did that include the owl?

I slowed as I approached the town square and parked in front of the abandoned hotel. Mine was the only vehicle on the block.

I crossed the street and scanned the dense branches of the tall spruce. I had not remembered the tree being so compact. This time it was a noisy place. Raucous grackles cackled and cawed and flitted in and out of the branches. The owl was nowhere to be seen. I would not have hung out there either amidst that cacophony. As I examined the branches of two nearby cottonwoods, I was startled by a boom of thunder. I hurried to collect a trio of thin brown cones from beneath the spruce. Another clap of thunder. I dashed for my car as the rain began.

I had been *in search of the owl,* but had known for some time now I did not need to find another actual owl. What I was discovering was *the wisdom of the owl...*insights about life and how best to live it. In this case, by its absence, the owl reminded me not to hang out where there is noisy, negative energy.

Sunken Gardens

As was my custom, I stayed overnight at the motel owned by my friends. I began my day's drive well rested. Within thirty minutes, I observed road signs pointing to Lava Hot Springs, a tiny town known, as the name suggests, for its natural hot springs. I seldom turned off there due to its proximity to my overnight stop. This time, something told me it was the thing to do. I had the luxury of time, not needing to arrive in Boise until late in the day; this time my dad was not waiting for me. The main street was lined with motels, shops, and other businesses, but the main attraction was the large hot springs pool.

Adjacent to the pool's manicured grounds was a labyrinth of paths and rock-lined flower beds. An intricate wrought iron arch spanning the entrance caught my attention. Its metal letters spelled out *Sunken Gardens*. That name reminded me of the sunken gardens in Lincoln, Nebraska that I had loved to visit as a child. But I had never explored *these* gardens. I parked my car at the curb.

I walked under the arch and began my descent along the footpath shaded by a line of spruce trees. They hid the garden from the road and the eyes of casual passersby. I followed the gravel path as it curled downward, hugging the base of a lava rock cliff that rose twenty feet above. There were numerous natural crevices in the volcanic rock. From a bench inside one of the nooks, I admired the diverse plantings: large red peonies with petals like crinkly tissue paper, yuccas with spires of still-closed buds, and pansy faces smiling in yellow and purple. A section of the path meandered under branches of cascading orange roses and past creeping phlox blooming in lush purple mounds. A mass of vinca groundcover had been allowed to overtake a steep slope, its vines accented with stars of blue blossoms. Shaded by the sentinel spruce trees, lily of the valley and graceful bleeding hearts were in bountiful bloom. I noticed two varieties of iris: one, a familiar deep purple, the other, heavily fringed in white-upon-white. Elsewhere, delicate pink and yellow columbine blossoms contrasted with the prolific hens-and-chicks succulents.

I also saw real animals: a patient hummingbird and a large yellow and black tiger swallowtail butterfly visited blossom after blossom. A robin made a brief appearance, and a sleek black cat with yellow eyes watched me intently, but tolerated my presence.

As I followed the winding footpath I marveled at the luxuriant growth of the garden oasis. On the adjacent hillside grew wild grass I knew only as cheatgrass. It looked tinder dry. I had discovered the garden at the optimal time. Later in the summer it would be oppressively hot and few plants would be at their best.

Satisfied with my garden visit, I exited through the metal archway, unlocked my vehicle, and drove the several-block-long main street until a display of metal sculptures caught my eye. I parked and ventured over for a closer look. Their intricate craftsmanship reminded me of the garden arch. I soon learned the artisan there had created both. I was drawn to a realistic sculpture depicting a great blue heron wading amongst cattails. Perched high on one of the reeds was a red-winged blackbird. I inquired as to the price: it was several hundred dollars.

I continued to browse, marveling at the many superb creations. Something kept urging me to buy the heron sculpture. I was certain it would fit in my Nissan Maxima. I talked to the manager again about the amount; this time I explained my idea of a memorial for my dad, a naturalist and inveterate bird-watcher. He reduced the price. I made the purchase. An assistant wrapped the sculpture so the four-foot-tall cattails would not vibrate and scratch each other as I drove. I adjusted the back of the passenger seat to be nearly horizontal. The package fit easily into my car. For the rest of the day's drive I had a new traveling companion. My plan was to donate the beautiful work of art to Hillcrest Retirement Center.

Now I understood: when I pay attention to the owl and my instincts, life unfolds wondrously. Something had drawn me not only to turn into town that morning, but also to visit the Sunken Gardens, so I would see the arch, so I would notice the steel sculptures at the shop, so I could discover and purchase the heron with the cattails and the red-winged blackbird.

Fortune Cookies

I reached Boise early on the eve of Father's Day. I had promised my dad I would return for Father's Day, and I had kept my word. The problem was, in the meantime, he had died.

My sister and her husband were to arrive later that night; my brother, not until morning. I welcomed being alone. The last time I was there we'd been occupied with the funeral, to say nothing of supporting each other in the early stages of our loss. There was a certain relief in being alone this time; I was accustomed to experiencing life that way.

I drove the circular drive into the retirement complex where Daddy had lived. His first-floor apartment was to the right of the entrance. I could see from the outside it remained vacant. The ponderosa pine that had provided a close view of nature from the window above Daddy's desk, and had shaded his patio and birdbath, had been cut down. He would have been deeply troubled by that. As times and life have a way of doing, change was afoot.

It was past suppertime. I decided to have dinner at the Golden Star, an Asian restaurant where Daddy and I had eaten a couple of years earlier. In later months whenever we drove by, his face lit up as he recalled our evening there.

The restaurant interior was just as I had remembered, including the elegant lantern-lights with heavy black tassels and the intricately embroidered wall hangings. I was seated at a small booth close to where my dad and I had dined. From the moment I decided to eat there, on my mind was my favorite memory of that earlier dining experience, which had to do with the fortune cookies brought after dinner. It had happened like this...

Daddy suggested I reveal my fortune first. I cracked the folded shell and pulled out the thin strip of paper. I glanced at it briefly and held it with two hands as I leaned forward across the table, smiling at my father and saying to him, "It says: *You are dining with a handsome gentleman who loves you very much.*" He smiled knowingly upon hearing the loving gesture of my obvious white lie.

It was his turn. Opening his fortune cookie and retrieving the message, he began. His voice bubbled as he said, "No kidding now... mine says: *You are dining with a beautiful woman who loves you very much.*" I laughed and smiled. That evening was a splendid example of our special times together.

Now tonight's fortune cookie had been placed before me. Would it provide a clue to my quest? Was I conferring too much significance on its message? I broke it open and ate a small piece of the bland but pleasant-tasting shell. The fortune slipped out.

It read, "Your dearest wish will come true."

Dearest wish. That would involve something precious. How and when would that heartfelt wish come true?

Five Days in June

The next morning, Lois, Robert, and I began our ambitious task of sifting through the stored items that had belonged to our parents. On the afternoon of the first day, we came across Dad's 35 mm camera in a storage unit with other items from his apartment. As opposed to magazines or clothes, this was an important item, a possession he valued and used often. The three of us were tossing out ideas of who should have it when I asked, "Is there film in the camera?"

My sister, who had overseen the transfer of the apartment items, had not thought to check. I picked it up. The answer was yes. I removed the film and volunteered to have it developed when I returned home.

We rented a truck to transfer items to be donated. Each of us set aside things of sentimental value or family history to keep. Our choices were affected by emotional ties, not marketplace value. Most of the furniture and larger household items had been sold at an estate sale after Mother and Daddy moved out of their home of several decades. That meant, except for the few apartment furnishings, we were dealing with smaller items, many of which had been boxed long ago and stored away for later. *Later* was now.

We worked non-stop for five days. Our shoulders and backs ached from bending over boxes and lifting item after item. We cried. We laughed. In our time together, we revisited many memories and made new ones. Finally our task was complete.

The metal sculpture was graciously received by the director at Hillcrest. By the time we were done with our project it had been installed in their serene courtyard garden. It stood beside a small recirculating stream that tumbled over natural rocks, exactly as I had envisioned when I made the purchase.

Headed home, I was alone again.

After the demanding dawn-to-nearly-midnight schedule of our days together, I welcomed the solitude of my drive. I spent much of the trip reflecting on the items, interactions, and insights of the past few days.

Granger

Somewhere in western Wyoming I passed a semi truck laboriously climbing a long hill. Trailing behind it was a substantial load of recreational vehicles. As I inched past, vehicle after vehicle displayed for me its model name. I read, "Adventurer. Adventurer. Adventurer." It was a welcome reminder of my dad's postcard greeting.

In all of my nearly fifty years of trips across the state, I had never driven the few out-of-the-way miles to tiny Granger to see its historic stage station. Wyoming is sparsely populated, so not to have visited a town so near the interstate seemed silly. This time, not knowing when I would be here again, I was determined to make that visit. I found Granger a town of perhaps one hundred houses, at least one-fourth of which were abandoned or in various states of disrepair. At one neat house surrounded by a manicured yard edged by a white picket fence, a grey-haired woman stood watering her lush lawn by slowly moving the spray from the hose from side to side. Despite the town's small size, the whereabouts of the fabled stage station surprisingly was not obvious. However, after a couple of ineffectual turns, I found it.

The stage station was constructed of stone. Considering the flat, sage-covered nature of the surrounding terrain, I wondered where the natural materials had been collected. Located at the intersection of the Oregon and Overland Stage Trails, it had been important in its day, also serving as a stopover for the Pony Express. Now simply small and nondescript, it gave me no reason to linger.

On down the street a bridge crossed a lazy stream. Along each bank of the waterway grew lush wild grasses. Beyond a couple of feet from the water's edge, they were unable to survive the dry climate. I parked my car and walked out onto the low concrete bridge for a look, certain I would discover something of interest.

Cliff swallows with their iridescent dark-blue topsides and clean wingspreads winged along the stream, catching insects within six to eight feet above the surface of the water. They careened back and forth, sometimes flying beneath the bridge, reappearing in droves. I picked my way down the steep incline from the roadway to the water's edge; what I'd hoped to see appeared many times over. Nestled against the concrete bridge in the ninety-degree angle formed by the horizontal overhang and the side of the bridge were the mud nests of the swallows. The rounded structures had been constructed one against the next, sometimes two-deep. I counted roughly two hundred nests along the east-facing side of the bridge, a mere eighty on the warmer and less-favored west side. Some were from prior years, mere skeletal outlines of the orbs of mud that once had been complete nests.

Curious to me was the habit of about three dozen swallows either entering or leaving their nests simultaneously. As I watched, I

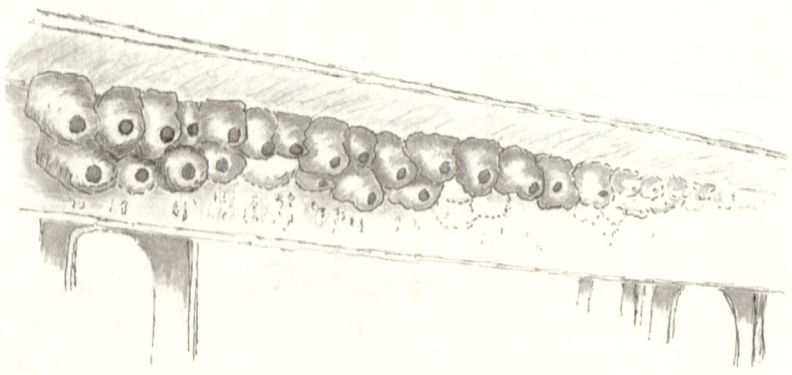

found myself not only in Granger, Wyoming, but also in Nebraska with my dad in May of 1999 visiting Cedar Point Biological Station. A biologist there, an expert on swallows, had shown my father his new publication in which he had referenced my dad's writing about swallow nests on the nearby, man-made Kingsley Dam at Lake McConaughy. My dad was excited to learn his early wildlife writings were still relevant.

I wished either the biologist or my dad were available to explain the phenomenon of the waves of swallows.

My dad had died. But by choosing to add the side-trip to Granger, not only had I relived one more memory with my dad, I also had satisfied a long-held curiosity about the tiny western outpost. With memories again as pleasant traveling companions, I returned to Highway 30 and headed east. I finally was headed for home.

June 30

I had been at work perhaps twenty minutes when Mindy called. She and Adam were at the hospital; her water had broken. She needed to stay in the hospital until their baby was born...by that evening, the doctors thought.

This was the day we had been waiting for. If I had butterflies, what must Mindy be feeling?

We kept in touch throughout the morning. I even arranged to leave work around noon for a short visit. Phone calls continued, updating me about the progression of the contractions. By late afternoon, her doctor predicted it was likely to be several more hours before the baby would be born. We agreed I would return to the hospital around seven.

The imprint on my parking garage ticket read 19:00, military time. It was exactly 7 p.m. When I reached their labor-birthing room several minutes later, the door was closed. I knocked hesitatingly. Within a minute, my son-in-law opened the door a bit and told me Mindy was in active labor. As we had discussed earlier, I waited outside.

The nurse who had been assigned to them all day spotted me in the hallway, recognizing me from my noon visit. She had just come off duty, so she proceeded to update me on the progress of the labor. She assured me that everything was going well and encouraged me to remain in the hallway outside the door. I thanked her, leaned against the wall, and waited, not knowing how many minutes or hours it might be.

Alone in the hospital corridor, I relived my own experiences with childbirth, especially the birth of my first child: my son. My pregnancy had gone well. I was excited to be having a baby. But there were complications during the full-term delivery. He didn't cry. They couldn't get him to breathe for several minutes. I lay on the delivery table shivering uncontrollably, not understanding what was going on. My tiny son, without oxygen for too long, survived only three days. Twelve months later when I went into labor with Mindy thirty days early, I was frightened. Now she was giving birth to her first, also a son. I waited, remembering the trauma of my own experiences, yet trying not to worry.

From beyond the door, a tiny but robust cry reached my ears. Tears of joy streamed down my face. My first grandchild had been born at 7:34 p.m. I continued to wait in the hall where I had received my precious gift: the sound of a healthy cry. The nurse had explained the baby would be brought out to be weighed soon after he was born. It wasn't long before Adam exited the room cradling his son, who was wrapped in a receiving blanket and wearing a tiny pink-and-blue striped knit cap. He motioned with his head for me to follow. It was at the scale I first saw him: a beautifully perfect, dark-haired baby boy who was *my grandson*. Without his swaddling clothes, he weighed six pounds five ounces. He was wonderful. Soon he was whisked back into the room to be reunited with his mother.

I waited awhile longer, thinking about the continuity of life: my grandfather Isaac, my father Levi, me, Mindy, and now my grandson. Although there were countless differences in our lives, each of us had experienced birth, the bright light of a new world, and someone to receive and love us, years and miles apart, and yet the same.

When the time was right, I was invited to join the newly created family of three. My daughter held her son close to her. He was cooing, making sweet newborn-baby sounds.

"So would you like to know his name?" she asked.

My mind was racing with anticipation. "Yes. What is his name?"

She beamed at him as only a new parent does, and said softly, "This is Samuel…" I heard every nuance of the utterance. It seemed to take several seconds to hear each tone of her answer. "…Samuel Levi." I had had no idea they were considering the name *Levi*. This little one had been given my dad's name. As I looked at my infant grandson, my head nodded a quiet blessing, my mouth smiled, but my eyes were moist with tears.

My daughter and grandson were doing well. Moreover, he bore my father's name. The fortune cookie had predicted perfectly. My dearest wish had come true.

Dry Creek

Mid-July. I was well overdue for a visit to Little Dry Creek, a usually tame waterway a couple of minutes' walk from my front door. Dry Creek is a misnomer. In my eighteen years here, I have *never* seen it *not* running, even in recent times of drought. A mere two to three feet wide, it expands to five in a few rare spots. Its usual depth, perhaps six inches. In my neighborhood it is a tidy stream that wends its way amidst slopes of lawn, groomed nearly to the water's edge. Yet it maintains its wildness, bubbling over rocks and depositing stretches of inviting sand in its bed. Grasses at streamside lean into the water, lovely tresses flowing in its gentle movement. Moreover, it meanders. I love that word, *meander*, its sound and all of its connotations. I first heard the term used by my dad to describe the stream in a valley at Rocky Mountain National Park. I was only five years old, but that word became one of my favorites. Dry Creek meanders. It curves this way and that, in no hurry to get to somewhere else, taking its time, so I am invited to take mine as well.

I had not experienced meditative time there since the previous fall. In the heat of summer, the ideal time to be creekside is soon after dawn on Sunday. The sun is behind the nearby trees and buildings, there are few people out and about, and light Sunday traffic on the adjacent street creates minimal noise.

I had set my alarm for earlier than usual. I arose eagerly. My favorite hazelnut coffee brewed while I donned a T-shirt and shorts. I stepped into the earliness of the day, coffee mug in hand, and headed for the creek.

The grass was still wet from overnight rain as I made my way across the lawn toward the creek. Air in the shadows was fresh and cool. As I approached the lip of the depression where the stream flows, I looked down. I was relieved to see I would be alone. I descended via a jumble of rocks at the steepest part of the creek bank. It had been my custom on prior visits to perch on a certain flat boulder because it provided a view far upstream. I was surprised to discover a fast-growing young cottonwood now blocked the line of sight from my familiar seat. Even here things had changed; I should not have been surprised. I selected a new rock seat closer to the water's edge. At my feet was a mound of fresh clover, its globe-shaped flowerheads a muted shade of mauve.

I was not early enough. The sun's strong rays had reached this section of the waterway. Before long the heat would be oppressive. For the time being, I sat quietly beside the creek; every few minutes I took a few swallows of my drink. I loved the quiet and the beauty of this tame little wild spot so close to my home.

A large gossamer-winged dragonfly hovered above the water, the iridescent blue of its wings glinting in the sunlight. Years ago my daughter had loved watching the magical dragonflies along the creek each summer.

The only evidence of bird life was the frequent call of a mourning dove, comforting in its familiarity. As a child I thought its name was *morning* dove because when my parents had identified the species for me, it had been, as now, in the morning of the day. Only later did I learn its name related not to a time of day but to the mournful cadence of its call.

I always learned from my early morning visits to the stream. This time its teachings were in the form of a simple, two-part lesson that easily could be applied to life: where the stream encountered apparent obstacles, it became more spirited...even musical; on the other hand, where equilibrium created calm, smooth water, there existed opportunities for reflections.

My own reflections continued. They all involved Little Dry Creek. On one of my father's last visits, we had stopped a mile upstream to observe the work of beavers which inhabit some stretches of this waterway. Another time, even earlier, my daughter had drawn around the outline of a creekside plant's shadow as it fell across her sketchpad. It was a creative technique I had never seen. On another occasion, she and I had waded in this same-but-different stream, enjoying the coarse sand beneath our bare feet. My eyes began searching the streambed for a future wading spot for Samuel Levi and me. The spot would go unused this year, but someday another generation would wade with me in this stream. Perhaps he, too, would delight over blue dragonflies.

I could tell when it was time to go: my mug was empty, the sun had changed from warm to uncomfortably hot, and I heard the rest of the day calling to me.

Birds in My Home

Nearly four months after my father's death, in place of frequent tears there existed a dull ache. I felt guilty when I didn't think of my dad for several hours. The desire to share news with him or to ask him about something arose less frequently. I was moving on down the road toward the realization my father was truly gone.

Although I tried to stay committed to the *search for the owl*, the midsummer record-breaking heat sapped my energy and withered my resolve. But spending less energy looking outward caused me to focus more on my home environment. I began seeing through different eyes, noticing anew the symbols of feathered friends that over the years I had invited into my house.

The birds I had observed in the past months had been true gifts, providing amazement, entertainment, guidance, and joy, thus nurturing my grieving spirit. As I focused on my various bird-related items, I realized they also could serve to salve my despondency via their connotations of beauty, freedom, and wonder. So it wasn't just that I was noticing them again; they were serving a new purpose as I connected them with the satisfying feelings of my recent sightings of real birds.

On my brass mail clip was the depiction of a goose; on the tissue box, a ring-necked pheasant. Seeing a pheasant the day of my dad's burial had provided joyful reassurance. Images of chickadees and goldfinches and nests abounded; a three-dimensional robin with a worm formed the base of a note holder. The robin in Mindy's backyard had been after a worm also. The brightly painted wooden plaque designed for me by an artist from El Salvador included a dove—not a mourning dove, but my mind readily made the connection. The Canada goose *Welcome* sign I had purchased in Pennsylvania for my dad hung near my front door. I once again saw the geese grazing in the park at dusk. A mug Daddy had often used when he visited bore a stylized quail. An inch and a half in diameter rotund robin crafted in Russia was one of my favorites. That ceramic was a gift from my dad.

A tree of life with silhouetted birds perched on its horizontal branches was depicted in my large Haitian cut-metal wall sculpture and in a Pennsylvania Dutch scherenschnitte (cut paper art) piece. The owl encouraged me to look up tree of life meanings associated with various cultures. In addition to the widely recognized symbolism of family, I learned the tree of life represents the interconnectedness of everything in the universe, as well as individuality—the unique human being molded by experiences. Whenever I glanced at either of the pieces of art, I felt a renewed sense of peace and understanding. I am not alone. And the very experiences with which I often struggle are creating the unique being I am destined to be. For the next several days, I took time to reflect on these reminders from nature that I had come to take for granted.

In my *search for the owl* I was continuing to discover its wisdom...this time as insights and understandings about the interconnectedness of all living things, the cycles of life, as well as the individual life. My life. My dad's life. Other lives. All connected and yet ultimately unique.

Void

It is easier to identify life's changes by looking back. For example, I remembered experiencing a heightened sense of anticipation after my dad died, awaiting connections that would serve as guideposts in my *search for the owl*. Sometime during the heat of summer, that excitement and sense of urgency withered. I didn't know when the change happened, but I ended up on an emotional plateau.

I experienced a new void. This one was not glaring, as had been the physical loss of my father. Emotions related to my loss were less painful; but somehow they were heavier. Lacking were surges of pure, spontaneous happiness. Life had a dull edge to it; I felt unable to cut through its tangled undergrowth.

My activities were simple. My conversations lacked their usual animation. Sales in my small gallery were lethargic. I made no plans. I didn't even want to write. However, this time of despondency was not to be dismissed. When I did feel up to it, the process of writing helped me continue to sort out my feelings.

Early one morning in still-too-hot August I went out to my tree-shaded patio to write. I was surprised to find the concrete strewn with yellow locust leaves, a sign of the approach of fall. Much as I had disliked the intense heat of the summer, I found my reaction to the dropped foliage surprising. Another change was coming. Tears filled my eyes. I had faced enough changes. How could I handle yet another? I wished, as I had many times this summer, that life would simply stand still for a while.

But the optimist in me knew change was normal, often for the best, and sometimes the only thing one can rely on. Thus the saying, "The only constant is change." Intent on trying to accept what I knew to be true, I proceeded to write about a lily that had graced the steps at the front of the church during the services for my father:

> The front of the sanctuary had overflowed with plants and bouquets. Afterward, most of the arrangements were taken to the retirement center where my dad had lived or the care center where my mom had died. The large double-stalked Easter lily, sent by friends of mine, I brought home in my car. The plant bloomed for several weeks. After all of the many buds opened, brightening my home with the symbol of hope, they proceeded to shrivel. I removed them, one by one, until all were gone. It was sad to witness the remaining leaves turning pale at the edges.
>
> Not wanting to relegate this plant to the trash, I relocated it to a shady spot on my patio. Knowing nothing of its growth habit or needs, I watered it periodically, keeping it slightly moist but well drained. Mostly it received my benevolent neglect. In midsummer, I was surprised and delighted when I discovered a new sprout of green lily-leaves

at the edge of the pot, a reassuring resurgence of life.

That was a month ago. I see another shoot has emerged. It is a gentle reminder that life and growth continue, with changes often emerging at unexpected times. I need that reassurance today.

I must be gentle with myself, let my tears drain, and await my own new growth.

Young Samuel Levi

Samuel and his family lived within three miles of my photography gallery, so it was easy for me to see him often: every day for the first two weeks of his life and several times during each of the weeks that followed. Some visits were brief, ten minutes or less when the timing was awkward. Others were for several hours. I helped the best I could. In turn, I benefitted from the dear connections. I loved the fact that by having a grandson, I had earned a new title. I was a *grandmother*.

Watching the rapid growth and development of any young being is fascinating. When it is your own grandson, it is absolutely awesome. At three weeks old, he responded to the honking noise of a toy bird. It bore the distinctive markings and coloration of a Canada goose. Soon after, I presented Samuel with his first bird book; page one featured a Canada goose. Thus, in harmony with my dad's love of birds, we initiated his namesake into the world of wildlife. Also in the book were a great blue heron and a red-winged blackbird. I hope someday Samuel Levi will see the metal sculpture of the heron we donated to Hillcrest Retirement Center.

The day he turned one month old, he slept two-and-a-half hours in my arms. I was settled into the large wooden rocking chair purchased before Mindy was born. Years ago, I spent many hours there holding her. Back in the familiar wide seat, I leaned against its comfortably high back with another babe in my arms. As I sat cradling my sleeping grandson, it was as though my need for time to stand still was being fulfilled. Samuel's first gift, given the evening he was born, was his robust cry. Now his silent sleep, its antithesis, was fully as welcome. Nothing other than my grandson had any claim on my time. He and I were together in a world of our own, sometimes breathing as one. When my arm became stiff, I moved it slightly, not wanting to wake him. He adjusted his little body accordingly. I lay my head back, not needing to think or plan, resting, and savoring the closest I could come to having time stand still.

Steady changes in *his* development served to move *me* forward. I was once again in the mode of watching and anticipating, my *search for the owl* having expanded to include what I could learn from Samuel. On the day he turned six weeks old, he favored me with yet another memorable gift: three effervescent smiles in rapid succession, smiles so spontaneous and beautiful his entire being and mine lit up with joy.

I wished that my dad could have been here to see his great-grandson's smiles. But he *had* seen his granddaughter Mindy for the first time when she was Samuel's age. Had she smiled for him that same way? Perhaps he had experienced that joy.

Wise Man and Vase

The first time I saw the work of art, it touched me deeply. I could have perceived its grey color as somber; it was, instead, calming and comforting to me. The skillfully hand-carved stone figure depicted an Asian wise man with a long thin mustache and beard. Standing two feet tall, he looked lovingly into my soul with his stance and demeanor, to say nothing of his kind eyes. My father may have been dead, but in my *search for the owl*, I had encountered another quiet, knowing man.

After several weeks of admiring it, I purchased the beautiful sculpture and brought it home in the back seat of my car. Because it was too heavy for me to lift, it remained there several days until someone helped me carry it inside. The venerable Asian found a home beside my houseplants, near the double-door to the patio. In that way, by looking beyond him through the glass, he also became part of my outdoor garden.

The presence of the silent elder was welcome reassurance in my world: a *something* I could see, that I could touch if I wanted to, solid and eternal. His right hand rested on a tall staff. His other arm was bent at the elbow; in his cupped left hand, he held a carved peach, the Asian symbol of longevity.

Juxtaposed with the art piece in my indoor plantscape was a globe-shaped ceramic urn with a rounded cover. It, too, was from

Asia, having been crafted in Vietnam; its graceful blue flowers were hand-painted upon a white background. The wise man stood guard over it, holding his symbol of longevity. I hoped his presence would serve to postpone the urn's eventual use: to contain the ashes of my remains. Whenever I glimpsed the two together, I smiled.

Recycling

As I was luxuriating in the rare circumstance of still being in bed at 7:30, my precious semi-wakefulness was interrupted by the noise of the ponderous recycling truck. Clatter of cans and bottles jarred me into full consciousness. Soon ideas began forming themselves into phrases, clamoring for me to be their scribe. I needed to write.

After brewing a pot of coffee and gathering my writing materials, I stepped outside. The recycling truck had provided the ingredients for the day's writing.

> Whether it was the frugality born of the circumstances of World War II, coupled with meager family income or the environmentalist natures of my parents, or, most likely, a combination of these and other factors, reuse and recycling were second nature to our family and still are to me. It's another part of my heritage of which I'm proud. As a whole, Americans throw away too much. I am glad recy-

cling has finally caught on, a reflection of nature's cycles.

 I paused in my writing to enjoy the pleasant summer morning and my surroundings. My patio plants were blooming profusely. More gold leaves had collected beneath the table. Already dry, they crunched beneath my bare feet. For today at least, I had come to terms with the impending change signaled by their falling. To the north, streamers of high cirrus clouds painted the azure sky. I quietly gave thanks to my dad for modeling for me all these years the appreciation of the nuances of nature.

The Last Photos

A month after our stint of dealing with Mom and Dad's belongings in Boise, I took Daddy's film in for processing, feeling sorry *he* didn't get to see the results. But we would treasure these photographs. How many negatives had he exposed? Would I know the *who, where,* and *why* of the subjects?

When I picked them up I was excited to learn the answers. Yet I waited until I was home to look at them. The first one was taken the previous November at my home. Happy memories of that morning with my dad swept over me. He had been excited to discover a fresh dusting of snow highlighting the pattern of the shingles on the roof of my garage. He took out his camera to capture the textures but it kept focusing on the dirty glass door. It was too 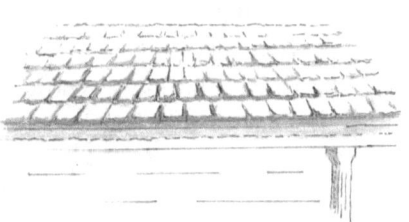 cold for him to step outside, so I washed the glass for him. We laughed about what it took for me to clean my windows. Each of the first three snapshots had the snowy roof pattern as its subject. For the third, my favorite, he had tilted the camera forty-five degrees to form an interesting abstract. I shifted it to the back of the stack. The next was of Mindy, Adam, Adam's mother, and me seated around the Thanksgiving table. I was pleased my daughter and I appeared in my dad's last set of photos.

The next one was astounding. Taken from the air, it showed a vast cushion of fluffy clouds. In the center, far in the distance, was a white protrusion, perhaps a taller cloud. I was puzzled about it, but not for long. The following photograph was of a pristine, snow-clad mountain peak surrounded by clouds. The next, one more mountain view. The top of the peak was flat, the identifying mark of Longs Peak in Rocky Mountain National Park.

Daddy loved the park and its lofty peak. In the summers during the late 1930s, he had driven a LaSalle touring car for the Rocky Mountain Transportation Company, carrying passengers back and forth from Denver or Estes Park to Grand Lake via Trail Ridge Road, a route that provided majestic views of Longs Peak. Mom had been employed in the gift shop at Grand Lake Lodge during those same summers. Over the years, I had heard many stories about their time working in the mountains of Colorado.

Three summers before he died, I had taken my father on his last trip over Trail Ridge Road. We stopped often to enjoy and photograph the spectacular vistas. He and I had stayed two nights in a rustic log cabin in Grand Lake. I had reveled in the personalized tour and his reminiscing about those memorable summers. All of this wondrous *remembering* swept over me as I studied these images of Longs Peak. In a manner I had not expected, Daddy was in touch with me.

The three mountain exposures had been made on December third, the day Daddy flew home alone after spending six days with me. I am thankful that for Daddy's last view of his beloved Longs Peak, it was photogenic, and he had captured it for the rest of us, forever. Daddy may have told me on the telephone that night he had had a great view of Longs Peak. Even if he didn't, it was the kind of thing he would have shared with me.

In the next photos Lois and Ted appeared on a January outing in the foothills above Boise, obviously with my dad. She, too, would be thankful for showing up in Daddy's last photos.

He had exposed the next three shots during my visit in February, less than two months before his death. Their subject was the wild turkeys we watched while visiting Al and Hilda at their mountain cabin. Each image focused on the four tom turkeys we had seen through the kitchen window.

So much for worrying about being able to identify the subjects in my dad's last photos; I was with him when he snapped the shutter on the majority of them. That was true for the thirteenth and final picture, shot later that turkey-watching afternoon as we drove the narrow dirt road that connected with the highway. The descending lane was bordered by tall trees; its curving edge defined by diverse undergrowth. Snow-capped mountains could be glimpsed in the distance. I remember the view and the situation well.

Daddy directed me to the exact stopping spot; in fact, I had to back up to the perfect vantage point through the trees, across the valley, and to the mountains beyond. I turned off the engine so he was free of its vibrations as he stood beside the car, steadying his camera against the open passenger-side door. He snapped the shutter one last time and we headed on down the road.

Five Months

After five months without him, I thought and talked less about my dad. Without knowing when or how, I began to allow the *now* of life to take precedence over the past. When I told someone about my dad's death, I summarized it in two or three sentences. The condensed version sufficed. It was as though initial wounds from the brutal impact of my loss had begun to heal.

Return to the Hospital

My daughter's thyroid surgery, postponed for several months because of her pregnancy, had gone well. By mid-afternoon she was transferred to a room on the fifth floor. An optimist like her grandfather, she was counting her blessings and expressing appreciation to hospital staff for the excellent care she was receiving.

Memories of the time I had spent with my dad when he was hospitalized with pneumonia intertwined with my experience with Mindy. Daddy's room and hers both had a northern exposure with treetops forming a far view. Each was located across the hall from the nurse's station, so the pluses and minuses of timely care and ongoing noise were ever at hand. The juxtaposition of the *then* and *now*, months and miles apart, intrigued me. When my daughter walked down the hall, it was as though I was watching Daddy walk down the hall with Mark.

While others took care of Samuel, I spent time with Mindy at the hospital for the two days following her surgery. I welcomed the opportunity to be alone with her. As my only child, my daughter has always been of paramount importance to me. Since my divorce, my mom's death, and now, the death of my dad, she and her small family had become more precious than ever.

Given the luxury of time, we chatted at length about a variety of topics. She reflected on the closeness she and her grandfather had developed in the latter years of his life. They corresponded sporadically but meaningfully via handwritten letters and phone calls. The interest he showed in her life had pleased her. She reminded me of a story I had told her a few months ago that demonstrated the memorable last example of his concern for her happiness.

On one of the early days of his final stay in the hospital, he and I were talking about the three-day cruise Mindy and Adam were taking. It was to be their final fling before the birth of their child. He had asked, "When did you say Mindy and Adam are leaving on their cruise?"

"Thursday morning," I had answered.

He knew how much they were anticipating that time together. It was late that Thursday, after they were off on their adventure at sea, that her grandfather died. I sensed he had not wanted to keep them from their long-anticipated experience, so I followed suit, informing my daughter of his death after they had completed their trip. How much did my father orchestrate the timing of his exit from this life? Did he choose when *not* to die?

My *search for the owl* had returned me to the hospital. Sitting quietly in my daughter's room as she rested between our conversations and her medical procedures, I sensed the presence of the owl, blessing the compassion and optimism flowing freely between Mindy and me. The last days with my dad echoed these promising days with my daughter. The two experiences complemented each other, with sadness and joy combining to create a hybrid emotion, undoubtedly some strain of love.

More Time with Samuel

Samuel Levi. I'd said or sung that name scores of times that day, a joyful day that was a welcome change from the ongoing challenges of grief. I spent the majority of the day with my grandson and daughter. Time with them was a source of great happiness.

At two months old, Samuel's little mouth curled up at the corners and he turned toward me when I sang made-up tunes, the lyrics of which were simply, "Samuel Levi," in varied tones and rhythms. More than my singing, he liked being outdoors. I'm unsure what he focused on, but he looked and looked, sighed his little sigh of satisfaction, and looked some more. Then he smiled at me. What a fortunate person I am.

What happened on this night was the best part of my day. Mindy and Adam brought Samuel to the reception at my gallery. I knew almost everyone, so I carried him from one person to the next, introducing little Samuel Levi and adding that Levi had been my father's name. To a few, I told the story of my dad's death. One by one, I connected others in this world with his namesake. I was fully alive again, thanks to the presence of my grandson.

As I held him, he drooled on the lapel of my black blazer. My daughter was embarrassed and apologetic. But I was amused, almost pleased.

After twenty minutes or so, the three left. I remained, enjoying myself late into the evening, proudly wearing the short trail of a dried milk drool, a grandmother's badge of honor.

PART THREE

Finally, Fall

Welcoming Another Season

And finally, it was fall. The hot summer had melted away upon itself; the refreshing crispness of cool nights contrasted with the warmth of glorious autumn days. I welcomed the changes and took time to reflect on the new season:

> *In my part of the world as the heat of summer wanes, subtle and sometimes not-so-subtle foliage colors clothe the landscape in rich yellows, oranges, and reds. The resulting vistas are bathed in the complementary, angular light of autumn.*
>
> *Autumn. Two seasons away from spring. Although my father had written that he loved spring the most, he valued aspects of each season and lived every day to the fullest. Now, memories of the pleasure and joy he found in life both comfort and engender profound sadness. As I reflect on his positive essence and acknowledge the reality of his absence from the earth he loved so dearly, I cry, sobbing*

softly on this quiet fall morning. This expression of emotion does not frighten me; it is sacred and honest. My tears, physical evidence of my connection with my father after nearly half a year, are gratifying to me. His strength and his attitude of joy have settled within me. My father, while no longer physically here, remains not only with me, but also in me. For all of this, I am thankful.

A lazy fly, still sluggish from the cool night, hovers only inches above my skin, buzzing loudly. I welcome its momentary distraction. I perceive the fly not as a nuisance but a tiny creature doing what flies are supposed to do. It returns, flying more energetically in zigzag patterns. I pause to marvel at its talent with regard to flight. As I watch the fly, I realize I have not seen a bird this morning in my garden. I understand fall brings changes in their habits; nonetheless, I miss the company of my feathered friends.

A siren wails in the distance. A bird chirps. I attend to the quieter sound from nature. What I automatically chose to do is what I learned to do over the course of many years. I'm referring not only to my observance of nature, but also to a greater gift: attitude and choice of where to direct my attention.

The experience of life is essentially about attitude. Henry Ford said, "Think you can or think you can't. You'll be right." How we look at a happening flows from perspective and attitude. It is difficult to identify an experience or event that does not serve a positive purpose even though sometimes its positive aspect is reflected in a larger context not initially obvious. The challenge is to look for the bright side of life and to focus on the gift of the experience.

Football Season

Fall is football season: another of my dad's favorite times. He did not possess a big frame but, because of his six-foot-two-inch height and passion for the game, he played on high school and college teams. He coached the sport for a few seasons during his early career as a teacher. Over the years, the love of the game stayed with him and he watched it on television with an eye for spirited, talented play. He admired finesse and innovative coaching and enjoyed following the development of a promising player or coach.

He watched football with binoculars at his side. Oh, he could see the TV just fine, but he was ready and willing to be interrupted at any time by a winged visitor outside his window.

I, too, am a fan. As I watch this fall, I intend to listen for echoes of my dad's voice accompanying those of the commentators, remarking on the jitters of the players as they try to gel as a team.

The cool nights revitalized the flowering plants in my patio garden. The impatiens that had supplied the garden with prolific but small blossoms throughout the summer generated brighter, pansy-sized versions. The late-season, long-stemmed florets of a hanging geranium bobbed happily in the breeze. Snapdragons I'd pinched back twice gathered the strength to produce a third round of flowers. For how many youngsters had my father demonstrated the opening of a snapdragon mouth? My daughter and me for sure, but someone else will need to show Samuel Levi. Perhaps it will be me.

One morning I discovered seven bright sumac leaves the wind had snatched from the neighbor's tree and deposited on my porch. I picked one up to examine it and could visualize my father doing the same thing, the long, gnarled fingers of his left hand positioned together but slightly bent to provide a spot to cradle the colorful specimen. He would have turned it over, pointed to it, or stroked it with his right hand. Within its soft-as-velvet surface, the sumac's yellow veins formed an abstract pattern against core colors of orange and red. The toothed edges curled slightly. My dad could have written an entire essay about this leaf as he did two years ago when he filled two handwritten pages describing a maple leaf.

Football. My garden. The changing colors of the leaves. Fall was upon me, providing a potpourri of wonders and triggering fond memories. The wisdom of the owl was gently guiding me; I was accepting of the path.

First Day of October

Three years ago on this date my father placed a brilliant red oak leaf on the stark white sheet folded across my mother's chest as she lay in bed, dying. Her shallow breaths caused it to rise and fall, rise and fall. Just minutes before eleven on that bright Sunday morning, Mother took her final breath, and the leaf lay still.

My father, sister, and I were at her bedside. We held her hands and told her we loved her. Then, to our surprise, several seconds later she opened her eyes and looked directly at each of us in a memorable good-bye.

My mother developed dementia several years before her death. At first, Daddy cared for her at their home. Later, daytime help was brought in to assist with food preparation and Mom's hygiene. Eventually, they moved from their home of nearly fifty years to a nursing care/retirement community. She lived in one building and he, in the adjacent structure. Daddy's deepest grieving over the loss of his wife came a few years before her death, when he lost her as a partner with whom he could share activities such as walks on the greenbelt with other seniors or time reminiscing. That initial grieving time had been challenging for him. He cried a lot. After the move he spent much of his time with Mom, but he also was able to resume some of the activities he had given up while serving as her primary caregiver.

Although they were born eighteen days apart, the manner in which they lived the final years of their lives had been in striking contrast. Mother lost her physical abilities one by one: her ability to remember, to walk, to speak, and finally...to swallow. Until his last twelve days, my dad had been immersed in life: taking organ lessons, working jigsaw puzzles, watching birds, reading, and writing poetry.

Each of the last two years on this date, after spending a quiet day, I had called Daddy on the phone. Connecting across three states, I had listened to him tell about his day and told him about mine. I couldn't call him anymore. Reflecting on Mom's death was bringing me closer to accepting his as well.

Mom's dementia and death were milestones for me. Throughout my adult life, I had remained in frequent contact with my parents. Mom's interactions with me were interwoven with words of worry or frustration and regret about many aspects of her life. It all affected me deeply; I wished things would go better for her. Her health was never great; she often had a physical complaint. She had strong opinions about everything. Dementia meant she no longer worried. Her complaints ceased and her limited communication was loving, often playful. She smiled a lot. Without her filters of worry and negativity, I was able to experience more clearly what I believed to be the essence of my mom.

My first loving act this morning was to water two plants that had been gifts at the time of Mom's death. Thankfully, they continue to thrive under my care. I also watered the African violet that originally had been Mom's, later nurtured alternately by my sister and my dad. It had been in his apartment bearing clusters of delicate pink blossoms when he died. As I poured several tablespoons of water into the saucer that cradled the flowerpot, I felt as Mom must have felt. All my life I had observed her doing the same thing. Often she carefully pinched off an old leaf or two or a spent flower. In the later years of her life, Mom's plants were instrumental to her mental health.

After lingering over breakfast and writing over several cups of coffee, I headed for the mountains, glad to have this day dedicated to my mom and me…and my dad. Along the highway, oases of stately cottonwoods ruffled their yellow-green leaves in the breeze. I was on another adventure.

Signs announcing a foothills park and trailhead caught my attention. In all my years living in the Denver area, I had never been to this place. I left the highway and after several turns, found myself at a large lot where half a dozen vehicles were parked. Wearing flip-flops, a denim skirt, T-shirt, and lightweight jacket, I wasn't dressed for hiking, but the day was perfect for an outing. The temperature was in the sixties; the breeze was cool but the sun felt warm.

I studied the extensive trailhead information and walked a hundred feet along the dirt trail and up a gentle hill until I could see the lay of the land. It stretched out gracefully in the hazy coolness of this first day of October. The subalpine slopes beyond were dressed in a mix of colorful grasses and outcroppings of scrubby two-to-three-foot vegetation. I needed to explore further.

The varied components of the foothills ecosystem pleased my senses. Immediately, two late-season white cabbage butterflies flitted past. A happy pair; I thought of my dear parents. Fluffy, low-growing blue-green sage begged me to pinch off a few leaves. I rubbed them between my thumb and forefinger to release their pungent aroma. The breeze carried the familiar chick-a-dee-dee-dee song of the tiny black-capped bird. The stately yucca plants bore wide-open seedpods, each comprised of three segments, themselves divided into halves. I gathered a handful of the shiny seeds, mature and brittle, and transferred them to my empty coat pocket. Where close-to-the-stem blossoms had decorated the eight-inch spire of another plant, fluffy white seeds had developed. I gently pulled off one perfect little parasol. I tossed it gently and watched it float away.

A few noxious weeds, Canada thistles, also were thriving on the hillside. Although their foliage and upper stems were withered, one or two of the intensely colored purple blossoms remained low on each plant, their colors more vivid than in mid-summer. Most prevalent on the hillsides were the delicate dried grasses of fall, reminiscent of the color of ripe oats. Here and there, flowering yellow composites decorated the terrain. The trail zigzagged up the hill. Red soil appeared close to a one-hundred-foot outcropping of similarly red rock. The stone sported attractive undulations and striations, polished smooth by nature. I left the trail to check out this inviting rock slab. I sat on its lichen-edged seat and leaned against the comfortably warm stone rising behind me. I turned my face to the autumn sun, thankful for the pleasant weather. I noticed something sheltered by a mountain currant bush—a healthy fir tree seedling. I noted the layers of branches and estimated the fifteen-inch-tall tree was five years old. That meant it had started growing not long before my mom had died. It was the only fir tree I saw on the hike. I felt a special connection with the handsome specimen. I hoped it would thrive.

As I stepped purposefully along the trail, a grasshopper startled me. I smiled, remembering the time when my sister and I were walking through a Nebraska field with our dad. My sister was tall for her age at six-and-a-half years old. I, however, was barely four; I was probably a little over three feet tall. As we walked through the field, with each step, we flushed scores of grasshoppers. They jumped not only against my arms and chest, but also right into my face. When my dad casually asked how I was doing, I answered, "Things keep jumping in my face!" Realizing my predicament, he picked me up and carried me, keeping me above the pesky grasshoppers until we returned to the car.

With my environmentally conscious upbringing, I needed no reminder to stay on the designated trail. However, the sight of the long, sharp needles on the flat, spiny pads of prickly pear cactus provided an additional incentive for me not to leave the path in my almost-bare feet. The cacti bore bright red fruit where yellow blossoms would have been in early June. I counted anywhere from four to fourteen plump red fruits on each plant.

As I continued along the gently ascending trail, my higher vantage point allowed a glimpse of a man-made pond, two acres in size, below where I had parked. In the calm surface were reflected tall autumn grasses that grew at its edge, grasses in warm hues of rust and amber and sepia. As I had several times earlier, I paused to jot a few notes on my tablet. The sun disappeared behind the clouds and the breeze kicked up. I continued walking.

As I gained altitude, upright junipers dotted the landscape. A striped moth lit momentarily on a yellow flower nearby. Small black pellets, probably droppings from a rabbit, had been deposited on one section of the trail. At the edge of the path, I spied a tiny wild rose plant, six inches tall. It was decorated with two perfect, bright-red rose hips. I'd never collected rose hips to make jelly, nor had my mom, but for some reason, seeing those rose fruits made me recall the delicious jams and jellies she had concocted over the years for our family. Her skill at all kinds of canning was amazing.

Bird sounds. A tiny bird too far away to identify called from the top of a juniper. Others played hide and seek inside evergreens, staying out of view but otherwise much in evidence. The sun was now but a brighter spot in a sky of grey. On the skyline above me was silhouetted a stark, graceful pine, resembling an overgrown bonsai and exuding Zen simplicity. Minutes later as the trail curved around, I saw it was an ancient ponderosa, sculpted by the prevailing winds. A clump of summer-green scrub oak grew at its base.

The trail twisted around a rocky hill, following the lip of a small ravine lush with densely growing scrub oak, mountain currant, and thin-leaved yellow-green willow bushes. The oaks were changing from green to yellow, but not yet red. In contrast, the dainty foliage of the currant bushes was vibrant in mottled green, pumpkin, and burnt orange. From within the dense undergrowth came the humming of a chorus of insects.

Remembering the red leaf on Mom's chest three years ago, I decided to pick two leaves to carry home with me: one, a scrub oak, the other, a mountain currant. I focused first on the small, irregular leaves of the currant. With many shades to select from and many attractive specimens, the difficulty was in narrowing the options. I picked a bright crimson, irregularly edged leaf, perhaps one inch in diameter. I held it gingerly between the thumb and forefinger of my left hand as I combed the low branches of the scrub oak with my eyes and right hand, seeking a sample to take home. This process was much more challenging; it readily became apparent there was no such thing as a perfect oak leaf. When I discovered one with no visual flaws, it lacked color; an orange and green leaf was torn at one edge; another flashed bright yellow but was brittle-brown around its perimeter. I recalled my dad's selection of the flawless, crimson oak leaf he brought as his final gift to Mother. Was it chance he had been able to discover such perfection for that singular event?

I selected a small one that was green and yellow, not without imperfections, but satisfactorily pleasing. I made a mental note: although no one leaf was flawless, together, they created a striking outcropping of scrub oak.

Beyond the ravine, the trail made a sharp hairpin turn and became steeper. My heart rate had quickened in the last hundred feet of my walk. The change in the trail told me it was time to retrace my steps. I had spent nearly an hour coming up, gaining a hundred feet or more in altitude in my walk of nearly a mile. As I descended I rounded a turn. From that vantage point, the pathway I had traveled stretched out below me. I traced it with my eyes, seeing the broad brown thread embroidering the light-colored terrain with zigs and zags. I was struck by how far I had come before turning back. That is true of life in general. Sometimes to appreciate how far we have progressed, we need to remember where we started. How was it I was able to travel so far? By taking, literally, one step at a time. No wonder others have written about this concept.

The sun slipped out from behind the clouds, causing my shadow to precede me on the trail. Finding my footing in the shadow presented a surprising challenge. I let my leg muscles instead of my momentum carry me down the often-steep path. A bright western bluebird darted across the sky and around the hill. A large butterfly, colored monarch orange and black, lit briefly on a broad, yellow flowerhead of rabbitbrush ten feet away.

On my descent I revisited the ponderosa. When I saw it against the background of the valley vegetation instead of the uncluttered sky, it was less than striking. Had this been my initial view, I might not have noticed its haunting Zen simplicity. What in life have I witnessed from a less-than-favorable perspective, and thus dismissed as mundane, when it was genuinely unique?

I rounded a low hill. Instead of birdcalls, I now heard noise from the highway far below. In the distance, the city sprawled for miles across the valley. The serenity of my nature walk was over. I pocketed my tablet and proceeded along the path to the parking lot. After scribbling a few reminders about my adventure, I drove off.

In nearby Morrison I stopped to eat lunch and look for a memento of the day. In a leisurely manner, I poked through the string of shops. In an antique store, I discovered an amber-colored glass lamp in the shape of a great horned owl. My *search for the owl* had led to...an owl. However, between the way it looked and the price, the decision not to buy was easy. In a garden shop I purchased a small, oval-shaped basin fabricated of iron. With two birds perched on its ivory-colored edge, it would commemorate this memorable day spent connecting with nature. A deep-red votive candle was my second and final purchase: signage indicated it was made from rosehips. It smelled like cinnamon, but it would be a happy reminder of the duo of red rosehips I spied on my hike.

I drove home, valuing the time to reflect on the day's happenings. I was grateful for all the memories of my mom and dad, some of them things I hadn't thought about for a long, long time.

At home, I checked my mailbox and discovered a slim package from my sister. Inside was a small book; the cover bore the image of a pressed leaf. On the first page she'd written: "A Special Gift to Jean from Lois, October 1." She also had been thinking of Mom and the leaf Daddy had brought her. The book was an updated version of *Leaves of Gold*, a compilation of inspirational quotes from many different writers on a variety of topics. Lovely botanical prints enhanced many of the pages. I allowed the book to help me open it, revealing a section called "Gratitude." I read several of the quotes, including:

> "So much has been given to me, I have no time to ponder over that which has been denied."
> —*Helen Keller*

and also:

> "It is a sad thing to reflect that in a world so overflowing with goodness of smell, of fine sights and sweet sounds, we pass by hastily and take so little note of them." —*David Grayson*

I recalled the slow pace of my hike and the feast for my senses. It had been a good day. Yes, an especially good day.

Not Yet

This first fall since my dad's death continued to be unseasonably warm. In a locale where it often snows in September, by mid-October we still were awaiting our first hard freeze. It had been gloriously gorgeous in the city, with the autumn hues of the trees and shrubs accented by blossoms of annuals and chrysanthemums.

When I arose from a sound night's sleep one morning, I peeked through the window coverings, as I often do, and discovered an autumn surprise. On the roof of my garage was a striking pattern of yellow leaves scattered by the night wind. The individual inch-long ovals, which had hung in neat lines on either side of a locust leaf stem, had been strewn randomly across the shingles, freshly minted gold coins glistening in the early morning light.

I stood in reverent silence, remembering my father's joy the morning he took photographs of the skiff of snow on this same roof. He would have reveled in this new display and reached for his camera. This time I preferred to capture it in my mind.

The concrete slab of my enclosed patio became the ultimate collecting place for the golden confetti that continued to filter from the overhanging trees. Soon it would be time to collect it into bags for recycling, but not yet. I wanted to continue to admire the colors and patterns of my secret garden, where summer and fall had joined efforts to create a new palette of colors and textures. Soon enough the killing frosts would vanquish the fuchsia-bright blooms of the geraniums and impatiens. Then would be the time to clear, to clean, and to prepare for another spring, but not yet.

My attitude toward many of life's changes can be summed up in those two words: *not yet*. I do not wish for change *not* to happen. I take my time with it, gaining some degree of control over it by being with it, allowing myself to feel it, and not hurrying it along. *Not yet*. It's my way of holding on while preparing to let go.

I follow Mother Nature's lead. She does not keep blossoms ever-fresh or leaves forever on the tree. But neither does she promptly prune her spent flowers or collect her shedding leaves. They remain to become seeds or to mulch against the winter's cold. She allows change, but in its own time.

The time will come to collect the leaves. The time will come when my nightly writings no longer overflow my desk. The time will come when I no longer display the postcard from my dad that begins "Dear Adventurer." Those times have not arrived. Not yet.

To the Mountains

I hadn't had a vacation since the death of my father. Traditionally I made the long drive to be with him in late spring and again in late summer or early fall. This year I had done neither. My grandson had become a primary focus in my life and I also spent considerable time writing. I was looking forward to an entire week in the mountains.

I'd been experiencing a deep-seated longing to reconnect with something gone from my life. At the core of my yearning was the desire to be with my father, to listen to his reminiscing, to watch his aged hands cradle a delicate leaf, or to look into his kind eyes once again as he said, "I love you, Jean." I wished I once again could experience his unconditional love. What I was feeling was not pain...simply a longing. Nature was nurturing to my father and me. I anticipated being recharged by the sweeping wildness of the Colorado high country.

The drive was enjoyable. The late-season sun highlighted the tired golden leaves of the cottonwoods, the streamside willows, and higher yet, the colorful aspen in valleys and hollows where wind had not blasted the trees bare. Elsewhere, on sweeps of windblown hillsides, the ivory trunks of the tall, densely growing aspen basked naked and proud in the October afternoon. The sky was a clear turquoise blue. The interior of my vehicle was becoming warm so

I stopped to buy ice cream: a single scoop of chocolate brownie fudge in a sugar cone. It was cold and filling, its chewy ingredients akin to a small meal. I drove on, savoring my ice cream and sipping the last of the coffee from my insulated mug.

As often happens on my first night in unfamiliar surroundings, my sleep was not sound. I arose early, looking forward to my first full day in the mountains and the arrival of three-and-a-half-month-old Samuel Levi and his mom and dad, to spend a couple of days with me in my mountain condo. I had finished my oats and first cup of coffee when they knocked on the door. Samuel Levi smiled at me. He exuded pure joy, his arms waving, his dimples displaying when he laughed. I took him into my arms. My daughter and son-in-law each claimed a spot on the over-sized sofa and began to unwind.

As we chatted and Sam took his morning nap, a sharp "Caw!" startled us. A jaunty magpie had perched on the railing of our small balcony. There are scores of balconies in this multi-unit lodge. How fortuitous that this flashy, long-tailed bird chose ours for his morning visit.

After Samuel Levi was awake, the four of us went out to explore. In the wide mountain valley to the south, we discovered large stands of aspen with their yellow foliage still intact. Wild grasses displayed a full palette of autumn hues: rust, pumpkin, oat, sage, sand, and olive. With a hint of a breeze, they began a slow waltz.

Mid-afternoon found Samuel and me together in a park. Another, or maybe the same, flashy magpie visited us, flipping through the dry needles beneath the nearby spruce tree. Its clown-like markings of white and iridescent blue-black and its quick movements caught Samuel's attention. As my dad had once upon a time whispered to me, I whispered to Samuel, "That's a magpie."

As the sun slipped behind the mountains, darkness quickly stretched itself across the valley. We enjoyed an evening fire, watching fingers of flame dancing in the fireplace. I noticed nuances of the flames I usually overlooked: tall blue spires tipped in yellow flickered above those of darker blue; quiet red and white flames hovered at the base. As though seeing through Samuel's young eyes, we three adults joined him in watching intently. In the past, time with my father had led to careful observation and appreciation of ordinary things and experiences. I was gratified time spent with his descendant and namesake was doing the same for me.

Early the next morning I went for a walk. The still mountain air was so crisp it stung my cheeks. My hands sought the enveloping warmth of the pockets of my short leather jacket. Above me hovered crystalline blueness.

On the horizon, skeleton silhouettes of densely growing aspen formed a skyward fringe. Their white trunks shone like clusters of matchsticks placed evenly upright as far as the eye could see. Elsewhere, deep-green conifers with lofty points were clustered on the steep slopes, their strong, needled branches ready to shed the inevitable snows of winter.

After a couple of blocks my route had me facing the unobstructed sun. While minutes earlier the morning air in the shadow of the lodge was harsh and cutting, once in the sunshine, my bare face felt comfortably warm.

My feet scuffed layers of nature's recycling: leaves, mostly aspen, in varying degrees of dryness and intensity of color. On the lookout for a few leaves to collect, I stooped to retrieve a shiny yellow almost-heart shape with jagged edges and a curving stem. I twirled it between my thumb and forefinger, causing it to quake as it had done while tree-borne. Two steps further I spotted a tiny specimen delicately patterned with orange and green, its veins a lighter yellow. A few yards beyond, my eyes found an aspen leaf of appealingly perfect size and shape, but sporting a dullish, pale yellow underside. When I turned it over, the morning sunlight reflected the gloriously brilliant waxy-gold essence of its top side.

The owl, with me on my morning outing, reminded me of a truth about patience and perspective: had I attended only to brilliance of color with my first glance, I never would have appreciated this superb leaf. I thought of the Zen pine. Remembering to reserve judgment until viewing things from many perspectives was an ongoing lesson…not only concerning nature, but also life.

Later that day my daughter and I, with Samuel in his stroller, were following a paved path beside the lively Eagle River as it tumbled down the valley. At one point, we, the path, and the river passed beneath a highway bridge. My daughter directed my attention to the scores of swallow nests on the beams above us.

There they were again…those familiar mud dwellings built neatly against the east-facing beam of the bridge, just as I'd observed them in Granger. First, my dad had observed, researched, and written about them. Next, I had discovered them. Now my daughter was pointing them out to me; were her little Samuel Levi a bit older, a fourth generation would be marveling at those master adobe architects.

We walked on. Neither what happened next nor my interpretation of it was surprising: a sudden breeze tenderly kissed our cheeks and caused tall, seed-heavy grasses to rustle. I had been *listening* for months. Was my dad passing nearby in the rustling grass, speaking to us?

At the River

The next day Samuel and his parents headed home. That afternoon I chose to revisit the beautiful untamed river.

Once there, the child in me took over. I ventured away from the shallow edge of the stream, maneuvering from boulder to boulder until I was halfway across the swift waterway. Having attained my lofty rock of choice, I crouched and sat, my chin nearly on my knees, my arms around my shins, hands holding my ankles...facing upstream. The tumbling of the water around and over the many rocks gave the river a voice that masked any man-made sounds. I welcomed the river's music as a backdrop to my quietude.

The water spilled effortlessly around my well-worn, granite perch. As far as I could see were boulders tumbled by time, smoothed endlessly by nature, and deposited into a random but pleasing pattern throughout the wide course of the shallow river. Ranging in size from eight inches to eight feet in diameter, they had in common their granite greyness and their semi-polished smoothness.

Sitting barely above the height of the water, the reality of the river's descent was more obvious than usual. A raft of rocks fifty feet upstream created rapids and a perpendicular drop of about ten inches. I marveled that these subtle drops, taken over the course of hundreds, perhaps thousands of miles, would allow these same waters to tumble down more than seven thousand feet to reach the sea.

I watched the water flowing around a nearby rock. The backwater on its leeward side created a small eddy. Therein was a four-inch circular pillow of ivory foam, slowly turning counterclockwise, adding clear bubbles around its circumference that subsequently climbed atop one another, contributing to its denser core. The creation reminded me of a delicate, tatted doily. It continued to pirouette, collecting more bubbles, yet never grew perceptibly larger.

On the far side of the creek, a substantial, rugged rock projected from the bank. Its decorative orange lichen added a boldly contrasting hue to the scene. Further along the shore, gnarled twists upon twists of exposed spruce roots created abstract patterns that continued horizontally for several feet, inches above the water. A sudden breeze stirred the air. I turned my head. Backlit by rays of sunlight, a rain of yellow leaves filled the air. After the sidewise flurry, the stream's silver surface became adorned with golden glitter.

A nearby willow whose narrow, pointed leaves were faded yellow-green attracted two active chickadees. They hopped from branch to branch. At times upside down, they played amidst the inner willow branches where foliage had been shed. Everywhere I looked the outer arms of deciduous shrubs and trees held most of the remaining greenery. In the cycle of growth, release, and rebirth, the younger, more vibrant leaves had the ability to hang on the longest into the Indian summer of October.

With the not-far-off freezing temperatures will come fanciful, crystalline ice patterns, first upon the shallowest of shoreline waters, then within the river itself, as frozen sculptures will form in the shaded areas of the frigid mountain stream. With snow, the orbs of granite will be transformed into magical marshmallows strewn amidst the thickly frosted landscape. As I sat there, an occasional chill breeze offered the sole hint of these cold-weather happenings. By the time this river world is dressed in winter, I will be elsewhere.

I cast my eyes downward, noting the mix of nature's odds and ends in this spirited waterway. Amidst the tumbled rocks near the shore were small stones wedged on edge and partially buried in water and silt, leaves in varying stages of decay, twigs, as well as rust-colored needles and paper-thin spruce cones. In the mud near the water's edge remained the paw print of a dog or some wild creature. I noted a single aspen leaf, showcased on a mid-stream pedestal of granite: it rested mere inches above rushing water that would eventually carry it downstream.

Then it happened…a slight burst of breeze, enough to cast the golden leaf into the turbulent waters. I watched it sink and be carried almost out of sight when quieter waters a few feet away enabled it to buoy its way to the surface, to ride a small eddy, only to be swallowed again as it encountered the next current of the energetic stream. It was a fight to the finish, with the delicate leaf no match for the powerful waters. Carried into the bowels of the rapid, rushing river, it could no longer be seen.

How unfair to the beautiful leaf…to have waved at the world from its high vantage point, soaking alternately in the shine of the sun and the moon, only to be released from the only existence it had ever known, and to drown.

Then I caught myself. My thinking was not in keeping with the nature of *nature*. The leaf was on its way to being recycled. And what of the brief episode of the leaf in the river? It need not have been a battle. Perhaps it was a playful dance between two disparate but willing partners.

Back Home

I was home. As I entered each room for the first time in more than a week, I saw through fresh eyes precious things that soon would become familiar again. The postcard from my father was on the kitchen counter, waiting for me. The rectangular glass case from the funeral had a thin layer of dust. From his portrait, taken when he was two months old, Samuel's wide eyes looked at me while the tiny fingers of his left hand grasped an imaginary something.

In the process of unloading my car, I scooted my feet through leaves. Their sound and smell reminded me of childhood. We kids had fun raking leaves into the outline of the rooms of a dwelling, complete with an entrance and openings between the various spaces. We teased one another when we forgetfully stepped through one of our imaginary walls. We may have created such "houses" only three or four times, but the etched memory is deep and clear. Memories: how curiously selective and fascinating they are.

The overnight forecast called for possible frost. Two plants on my well-protected back patio deserved to be brought inside for the season. Both had been gifts at the time of my father's death: the first, a brilliant fuchsia-colored geranium in a cobalt blue pot, the second, the Easter lily with four new shoots. I placed the geranium on my kitchen counter where it would receive morning light. I paused to enjoy the slightly fuzzy, irregular leaves and their peculiar geranium scent.

I returned to the patio for the lily. At first glance, I thought its top-heavy growth merely warranted a stake. Then I saw them: three slender flower buds nestled within the floret of narrow leaves at the top of the tallest stalk. It was a homecoming gift without equal. I carefully lifted the large plastic pot, allowing the lily plant to rest against my upper body as I transported it into the kitchen. I placed the plant where it, too, would be bathed in morning sunlight. The lily, symbolic of resurrection in the Christian worldview, had itself come back to life in only six months. Its stamina and beauty touched me deeply.

My father could not live forever. Neither will this lily plant. However, continuity and perseverance of life were expressed well for me in this one living symbol. It was a striking reminder, not of death, but of the miracle that is life.

Reading His Books

Among my dad's most treasured belongings were his books. Much as he loved to write, he also was an avid reader. When my sister, brother, and I convened to make decisions about his belongings, scores of books awaited us. These favorite tomes had followed him from his home of nearly fifty years to his small retirement apartment. Housed temporarily in a storage unit until we came together to sort them, they filled several boxes.

Some books bore inscriptions by my father, designating who was to have them after he died. The majority held no notations. Most were nonfiction and related to his passion for, and work associated with, nature and the environment. Authors included Aldo Leopold and Olaus Murie, my father's fellow environmentalists. There also were books he had authored. We three took turns selecting books. My sister had a strong connection to the thin brown one from which our dad had taught her the names of ducks when she was a toddler; it is now hers. The process took a long time as we perused the well-worn hardback volumes, long-familiar friends to our father.

I had selected *One Day at Teton Marsh* by Sally Carrighar; I can't remember when that book wasn't around our home. The inscription on the inside page, in my mother's careful script, explained why. It read:

December 25, 1947
To Levi
From Luella

The title of the book had always appealed to me, as did the tattered yet attractive rust-colored book jacket with its large black-and-white illustration by George and Patritia Mattson. The graceful, realistic image, portraying an otter and Teton marsh, originally had been rendered as either a woodblock print or pen and ink sketch. For me, it always has been a comforting image. I added others to my stack, including Daddy's *Field Guide to Western Birds* and a small, well-worn copy of *Field Book of North American Mammals*. The latter bore a 1928 copyright and, on the inside, addresses of three of his earlier residences. The first two had been crossed out. Although he had not lived at the third location for many years, the list had never been updated.

Once home, even as I ceremoniously transferred them to my bookshelves, I did not take time to open most of the books. Eventually I was moved to act, for some of these books I knew only by their covers and the warm association with my dad. I decided after all these years to read *One Day at Teton Marsh*. Author Carrighar's descriptive, imaginative prose, based on well-researched information relating to each inhabitant at the marsh, made for engaging reading. It also provided a welcome connection to my father: my eyes were skimming the very words his had read many years ago. There was comfort in being immersed in his much-loved literature. I looked forward to reading more of his favorite books.

Something Missing

When I left work one evening, it was after sunset...that magical time we call *dusk*. Heading unhurriedly to my car parked a block away, I was enjoying the softness of the air and the evening light. Even before I saw them, I heard them: Canada geese honking as they flew overhead. I stepped to where I had an unobstructed view of the dozen or more graceful birds. They flew majestically; the group's striking V-formation silhouetted against the sun's afterglow. But something was not right. There was a large space between the lead goose and the second goose on one leg of the *V*. That position in the formation was conspicuously empty, akin to the solemn *missing man* formation of jets honoring the memory of someone who is dead or missing.

Something in the grand pattern of nature *is* gone. That something is my dad. By the comforting call and the sinuous, familiar flight of the geese, I was once again reminded. I remained still, taking in the profound message. The geese, one seemingly missing, had honored him in an eloquent manner while affording me an opportunity to revel in the simple beauty of their striking twilight flight.

A Serendipitous Occurrence

By mid-November, I was struggling to adapt to the shortened hours of daylight. And I wasn't the only one. The tall lily-spire received minimal sunlight in my kitchen. I sensed it, too, missed the luxury of long hours of daylight and warmth. Straining toward the precious rays, it continued to grow; the spire was twenty-three inches tall. The third bud became stunted and fell off. Buds one and two remained tightly closed and pale green in color. Having withstood more than three weeks of being indoors, they still showed promise of flowering.

I continued to water and to watch my resurrected lily plant. When I arrived home late on the evening of November 17th, I checked the plant before retiring for the night. Bud number one, promising to be the first to open, was still tightly closed. I switched off the light and went upstairs to bed.

I arose early the next morning. The day promised to be a full one. Once downstairs I glanced at the lily. Satiny points of six white petals had parted and a perfect flower was beaming at me. A wondrous sight…and a serendipitous occurrence. In a few hours, my brother, his daughter and her husband, plus my daughter and Samuel, would arrive here for lunch. Was it a coincidence it was today, the first time a family group of this size had gathered in my home since Daddy's death, that the lily chose to open? I only know it was magical...as though Daddy's essence was truly with us. Nature had found a way into my home to bestow its blessing. I moved the lily into the dining room when we gathered there to eat. I eagerly shared its story with the others.

We spent our time catching up on family news and watching little Samuel. This was the first time he had met his great-uncle Robert.

Samuel Levi's favorite aspect of his visit to Grandma's house was the antique wall clock in the living room. It talked to him, saying "tick-tock," and its swinging brass pendulum waved back and forth at him. He was fascinated by it and strained his neck to watch it from any part of the room.

Samuel's fascination with the timepiece heightened my awareness of the symbolism of today's happenings. There clearly existed in my home the continuity of time: past, present, and future. The lily, a gift at the time of Dad's death, was blooming at the perfect time, its blossom the symbol of resurrection and hope. And there was four-month-old Samuel Levi, with most of his life lying in the future, watching the pendulum of the clock as it swept moments of the present into the past. Poignant feelings deep within me were providing an experience mere words could not express.

Grandpa's Greatest Memories

Shortly after my daughter was born, I had given Daddy a hardback book titled *Grandpa's Greatest Memories*. The pages were blank, designed to capture a grandfather's writing for a grandchild. When my father died the book contained nine short essays and one poem, all in my father's familiar hand. The original would be Mindy's but since there would be no more additions to the book, the time had come to have copies made for his other grandchildren. Gifts for our special Christmas.

Tucked among the pages were originals of each of the writings along with various notes and a small piece of paper bearing an outline for another book. Evidently my dad had intended to compile a more extensive body of work: some of these essays along with more of his writings. I had not known of his plan until that discovery. I must try to locate those writings and put together the collection he had in mind.

The notes and loose, edited writings were removed for safekeeping. I departed to run my errand. My route to Kinko's took me past the park with the gnarled willow. A flock of Canada geese was circling overhead, counterclockwise, I noted, no doubt preparing to land on one of the ponds.

After ordering spiral-bound copies of the book, I returned to the park. There was a bracing quality to the late afternoon air. I made my way to the vicinity of the willow. I couldn't help but notice a vine nearby, for in the spotlight of just-before-sundown rays of light, the last crimson leaves of the season were afire with color. Stillness pervaded the place that had become important to me, where I felt not only closer to memories of Daddy, but also more in touch with my *search for the owl.*

The shedding of the willow's thin leaves had revealed a chunky nest two-thirds of the way up the sprawling tree. I scanned the leaf-strewn earth below. No small creatures were braving the chill of late day. Nor were other human visitors here on this Friday afternoon. The sun disappeared below the horizon, trading places with the approaching dark.

I said good-bye to my friend the willow and walked briskly back to my vehicle. I drove to the south end of the parking area to obtain a view overlooking the narrow pond some ninety feet away. In its quiet water a solitary waterfowl was swimming directly toward me, trailing a silvery *V* across the otherwise glassy surface. As I stopped the car to watch, it paused also. The V-shaped wake disappeared. Effortlessly, the duck became airborne and flew directly toward me. As it approached, it dipped slightly in its flight path, passing less than ten feet above my car. My heartbeat quickened. My skin prickled. It...or was it my father...and I truly had been in touch.

Thanksgiving

Thanksgiving. It is the name given to an autumn holiday. In the larger context, *thanksgiving* is a noun connoting the act of giving thanks. On Thanksgiving Day I put my gratitude into words.

An attitude of thankfulness pervades my being today on this the fourth Thursday in November. There is much for which I give thanks: health, family, and friends; worthwhile activities; comforts of an adequate income and a cozy home; and memories, to say nothing of the ability to remember. Having experienced my mom's plight with dementia, I appreciate my still-intact mind.

Last year at this time, my father was in Denver. It was at that Thanksgiving dinner he talked about being thankful for life. His words continue to fascinate me. Each living thing is dependent upon another for its existence...and the subsequent interde-

pendence with other living things creates the complex environment in which all things exist. The capacity for life...be it human, plant, or animal...is phenomenal.

My father's death makes more precious his having spoken about life. At my Thanksgiving meal today, I, too, will give thanks for life, especially for that of my grandson.

He and Mindy and Adam are in Atlanta today. I am finding pleasure in a quiet day to myself. Nearby, the lily's now two perfect flowers smile at me. The wall clock tick-tocks patiently, rhythmically, in the next room, as steadfast as a good friend.

I am thankful also for today's sunshine and blue sky. Hanging from the garage eave, the ivy geranium's dry leaves and tendrils cast a cavorting shadow on the wood siding. A breeze tosses the arms of the bright-hued windsock. The shadows and the windsock are pleasant companions this afternoon.

One fall, in addition to the two-page piece about a maple leaf, my father had written a shorter essay (now in Grandpa's Greatest Memories) titled "Two Golden Leaves." When I read it a couple of days ago, I was amused that his observation of the last two leaves on a lilac bush included the fact they were at the tip of the tallest branch, echoing what I had noted on my mountain outing. He went on to write:

"...a further look at the same bush made me realize that when one season is ended another is sure to follow, for every branch ended in a well-formed but compact bud which would remain quiet until the warmth of spring would stir new growth.

"A bush isn't really ending its life when freezing nights come, because it is already organized to bring us the new leaves and blossoms of the coming year. The gold of fall is sort of a celebration for a task well done, but the buds which are already there are a promise for spring."

I am thankful my father was a prolific writer; these words are comforting to me. It is as though he had been writing about our family lineage and its next descendant. Yes, before he died, things were already organized to enable Samuel Levi to come into this world. What promise his young life holds.

Later That Day

I reflected more on the events of the previous year when my father was in Denver. Thanksgiving night we had placed paperwhites in a shallow brass bowl. I had watched my dad's broad fingers carefully place the bulbs, nestle them in moist vermiculite, and cover them with smooth river rocks I had collected from a local streambed many years earlier. Tonight I again performed the many-year-old narcissus-planting ritual. However, this time I was preparing two containers: the second was for Mindy.

Once the planting was complete, I cleared and dusted my narrow fireplace mantel. From the basement I retrieved the holiday wall hanging and a medium-sized box marked with a Santa sticker.

I unrolled the latch-hook hanging depicting Santa's smiling face. My daughter created this piece when she was twelve years old. Each year when I view it for the first time, I am amazed at the precision with which she fashioned it, evident in the evenness of the plush surface. My dad also had admired it. As I had done for many years, I hung it on the wall above the fireplace.

I unpacked my Santa figures, arranging the eclectic collection of more than a dozen on the mantel. Last year Daddy had exclaimed over each one: the whimsical gourd from Tanzania painted so the seated Santa's legs crossed beneath him, Father Christmas in traditional dark red velvet, the hand-carved wooden Santa I had purchased in Oregon, and the cylindrical box designed to hold fireplace matches, but decorated as a Santa. My father's interest in each item pleased and surprised me.

I asked, "You haven't seen most of these things before, have you?"

"No, Jean, I haven't been to your home for the holidays since 1973." (Of course, he knew the year.) "I think next year I should come to your place for Christmas."

That comment set in motion an entire year of anticipation of this year's family Christmas. What we failed to consider was that before that event, Daddy might die.

More Letting Go

Several days after Thanksgiving, I was seated at the dining room table noting the light streaming in through the sliding glass doors. I glanced at the lily plant, also basking in the sunshine. A closer look confirmed both blooms had withered. It was time to remove them from the plant. To cut off the duo of shriveled flowers was to acknowledge again that my father and mother (for the second one had become symbolic of my mom) truly were gone from this earth. I was encouraged that several more slender sprouts had emerged since the pot had been indoors.

I took my garden shears and snipped cleanly through each of the two fat flower stems. The petals were tissue-dry, brown and unsightly. Placing them into the kitchen wastebasket was difficult. But even for me, the inveterate sentimental saver, saving them made no sense. Moving them on was another step in my process of growth and healing. The owl was continuing to share its wisdom about life. And death.

Preparing for Christmas

Soon much of my time was devoted to holiday preparations. Physical indicators of Christmas continued to appear. The narcissus shoots straightened and began their upward push. Seven poinsettia plants sat nestled in their foil-covered pots on my coffee table. Some were to be gifts; others were for me.

A white poinsettia with deep-blue foil wrapping and silver ribbon would be an early Hanukkah gift for my daughter's family. Although Mindy had chosen to convert to Judaism, the faith of her husband, before their baby was born, they still planned to participate in many of our Christmas activities. The need to increase my understanding of the Jewish religion and customs was yet another change confronting me.

I had ordered two sets of Daddy's last photographs. I planned to insert them into small albums for my brother and sister. Even though he had died, Daddy was helping me a lot with my gifts this Christmas.

I wrote a holiday letter to enclose with my Christmas cards. In recent years my letter, sent to friends with whom I communicate only at the holidays, had been interwoven with accounts of the year's adventures with my dad. In fact, I began this letter with the highlights of my trip to celebrate Daddy's ninety-fourth birthday. I shared the news of his death and the birth of my first grandchild.

What news will be included in next year's letter, without my dad to write about? In addition to an update about Samuel Levi, what else will I have to say?

Late one evening, something surprising happened. I was sipping a glass of cabernet. I was relaxed and happy; it had been a full and productive day. Nonetheless, as I thought about my dad, I began to cry. My tears flowed freely. I sobbed. I moaned and wailed. I produced drawn-out, sustained screams. The sound hurt my ears, but the strain on my vocal chords was strangely satisfying. The physical effort it took to express my emotional pain in that manner was new. My body was taut. I used every muscle to maintain the primordial shrieks. Although I had cried a lot the night my dad died, it had not felt like this. Tonight the force of my feelings and the excruciating decibels of my outpouring astounded me. I was not drunk. The wine had relaxed me enough so I could express in an animalistic way what had been buried within me for months. Eventually, exhausted, I slept.

The next morning I awoke cleansed and at peace. It was as though I had achieved a balance point deeper within me. The honest, physical expression of the pain of my loss had been cathartic. Why had it taken so long for this to occur?

I was ready to move forward, still missing my father, but with a clearer understanding of how important it is to express grief. For several days, everything I attempted was easier for me. My brain functioned more clearly. I felt whole. By letting go, I had gained more of myself.

The Equalizer

The forecast was calling for snow. I consider snow to be the supreme equalizer, enveloping and decorating identically both the trash and the treasure of the land. I love to watch it snow, to see the white stuff collect, adhering like plaster if wind-driven, or piling to amazing heights if it arrives fluffy when the air is still.

The time was finally right. Having shed their leaves, the trees stood ready to bear the weight of the white precipitation. There had been little rain this fall. The thirsty land would welcome the moisture.

It began as slushy drizzle in late afternoon but soon turned to fine snow. It was the kind of storm that can settle in for a long visit, with enough wind to clothe tree trunks in garments of white. I watched as something developed once more: the patterning of the shingles on my garage roof, highlighted by the falling snow.

Storm, Tears, and Gingerbread

I heard the wind howling in the night. I knew the brunt of the storm had arrived as predicted. When I eventually awoke for the day, I rolled over and peeked through the blinds. More snow. I lay in bed, listening to the wind. As I usually do before rising, I began to envision the activities of the day. Today's *Plan A* had been to head out early to select a Christmas tree. Given the near-blizzard conditions, I needed to develop *Plan B*. I decided I would start by setting up my gingerbread village on the dining room buffet. I scooted myself a bit further under the comforter, cozy in the warmth of my nightlong space. I imagined myself carrying each gingerbread creation from the basement and carefully removing it from its plastic bag.

I also thought of my father and his intention to be with me at this magical time of year. Christmas...when talk of angels and miracles is accepted, when expressions of love are encouraged, when both giving and receiving are common. I imagined how delighted he would have been to see the four structures Mindy and I had put together with frosting.

My positive, flexible attitude was giving way to disappointment on this dark morning. Feeling defeated, I wanted to stay in bed. Tears filled my eyes. As the wind cried outside my window, I cried as well. It was not supposed to have been this way. I was supposed to have been arranging the gingerbread village for my dad to enjoy. Oh, others would enjoy it, but *he* would not. And *I* would not experience my dad's sincere, appreciative comments.

Eventually I got out of bed and began my day. I brewed a small carafe of hazelnut coffee. I opened the kitchen blinds. The tree branches were blown free of the dry stuff; they rattled like skeletons in the stiff, sustained winds. The snow had let up yet the cloud-filled sky was as white as the ground, a stark canvas highlighted only by the bleak harshness of the bony trees.

Then I saw it. A squirrel, no doubt hungry after a near-zero night, was clinging to a branch of the locust that grew beside a Russian olive outside my patio fence. Outer growth of the two trees intertwined. On this windy day, the squirrel had figured out that the strength and stability of that branch was a better place to be than the more spindly, flexible branches of the Russian olive. Yet it was the Russian olive that bore an abundant breakfast for the squirrel. I watched as this resourceful creature feasted on dry Russian olives while hanging by its back feet from a swaying locust branch.

Even before my own breakfasting, I made room for the gingerbread village. I moved the rectangular glass box with its mementos and dusted and polished the exquisitely grained wood of the oak buffet.

It was time to retrieve the small creations from the top-most storage shelf. I carried each one carefully, unwrapped it, and positioned it on the buffet. I added a miniature fence in front of one of the houses.

My father had seen the oldest of the four structures in 1973. Its once-white icing has yellowed; the red-and-white candies are faded. Yet miraculously, it has survived. The other three were created either by or with my daughter. One was a small house she made. The other two were joint projects: a church with stained glass windows made of sugar candy and a one-room schoolhouse complete with front ante-room and cupola tower and a miniature metal bell that actually rings.

Through the ritual of positioning the structures and recalling memories associated with their creation, my energy had been renewed and my joyful anticipation of the holidays rekindled.

The Christmas Tree

The season was still officially fall, but only one week remained before Christmas, our special, long-anticipated Christmas. I had purchased the tree three days earlier. Now it was time to adorn it with my eclectic collection of ornaments.

My daughter and Samuel arrived about 8:45 in the morning. I was grateful that Mindy was willing to devote her day and Samuel's to helping me. In recent years, decorating the tree often had been a slow, solitary activity.

When the furniture had been rearranged, I carried the tree in from the garage. It was a sheared Douglas fir; it smelled heavenly. Samuel watched us from his bouncer chair as he experimented with varied sounds. While Mindy held the seven-foot evergreen upright, I lay beneath it, guiding the trunk into the wide stand. It took us five or six tries before it was centered and secured. I rolled out. Mindy and I stepped back for a look. We laughed. It was far from vertical. I crawled back under the tree and readjusted it. We stood back for another look. Much better. What must Samuel have thought about our unusual behavior, especially his grandma crawling around beneath a tree?

I threaded the multi-colored lights in and out among the dense branches. Samuel was fascinated. Strains of "The Nutcracker Suite" were coming from the CD player. When I moved my armload of plugged-in lights to the rhythm of the music, he squinted in pleasure and squealed with delight.

I had been looking forward to sharing certain tree-trimming rituals with him and with Mindy. For example, I wanted him to see the large, delicate NOEL ball, purchased when Mindy was almost a year old. Since *Noel* is Mindy's middle name, it had become her favorite ornament. Because she is Jewish, it continues to find a place on my tree. Its clear glass captures the multi-colored lights. I took pictures of her showing it to Samuel.

The decorations kept emerging and finding their places on the tree. Eventually I came to the small stuffed bird, handmade from red felt and embroidered in white thread. I had created it the year before Mindy was born, the December I was expecting my first child. On the evening of Friday, December 13th, as I finished the final embroidery stitches and prepared to hang it on the tree, I began to experience labor contractions. A little son, born later that night, died three days later.

Every year the bright cloth bird receives a place of honor high in the front of the tree, a tribute to baby Ryan Matthew. My infant son had been one of my greatest teachers: guiding me to discover an inner strength I had never known.

My daughter was holding Samuel Levi as I lifted the red bird from its box. I held it out to Samuel for him to see. He looked at it painstakingly. This dear being studied the bright decoration, then reached out and took in his hand not the bird, but my forefinger, grasping it firmly and lovingly. I believe he knew. His wise soul knew. No words were spoken. Something wonderful was happening. After perhaps thirty seconds, Samuel released his grip. I turned and hung the ornament high on the tree.

Finally I unpacked the last item I had been looking forward to sharing with Samuel: my matte-finish white angel with her two thick braids. I gave a slight twist to the music box key in the pedestal base, so the tune would play slowly for Samuel, and he could watch the angel's measured rotation. I held her close to him; he listened and watched attentively. It was a tender experience.

However, at the same time, I was having an experience I had not anticipated. I had forgotten what tune the musical angel played. As Samuel Levi listened, in my mind I was hearing the words to the tune: "Sleep in heavenly peace, sleep in heavenly peace." The music took me back nearly nine months, to my desperate drive of hundreds of miles through the dark of night, determined to see my dad still alive. It had been early spring, yet I had played Christmas carols as I drove...music I had hoped I would be sharing with him this holiday season. The selection that had moved me to tears as I drove, taking on a new meaning, was "Silent Night," in particular the phrase "sleep in heavenly peace." I had wondered, "Is that what death is? A forever sleep, in a heavenly peace?"

Yes, my dad had died. While Mindy and Samuel listened with me, the carol was here again, this time being played by the simple, precise tones of a music box: "Sleep in heavenly peace, sleep in heavenly peace."

PART FOUR

Winter Awakenings

First Winter, Then Christmas

It arrived at 12:04 a.m. on December 22nd under cover of a dark night: winter, another season to experience without my father. I was relieved in some ways, knowing this was the *final* season to face anew without him. Soon after the onset of winter, my family would gather to share the festivities we had anticipated for so long. Soon it would be Christmas. The *Grandpa's Greatest Memories* books and photo albums would be unwrapped. Samuel would experience the musical jack-in-the-box I had chosen for him.

The fragrant narcissus blossoms had begun to open several days before. I had purchased a new glass ornament depicting an owl. I hung it beside the red "baby Ryan Matthew" bird, high on the tree. Soon both birds would be eyeing a house filled with relatives building new memories.

On December 24th, Lois, her husband, Ted, and my brother, Robert, arrived. They would be in town for a mere four days. Lois brought a couple of additions to our holiday celebration. The first item was for me: a small packet of tissues. She had written, "To JEAN, From LOIS… Just in case…I shed a few tears wrapping presents." She also brought paper plates and napkins decorated with poinsettias, ones she had set aside when Mother and Daddy's house was sold.

"Thanks for bringing them," I said. "Let's use them tonight for our sweet treats."

"Perfect. Thanks."

Other family members joined us that evening in my intimate townhome. We began with Lois, Robert, and me sharing childhood memories of decorating our family tree. This was often done on Christmas Eve. Lois explained it had happened that way because Daddy had been away from home until a day or two before Christmas, involved with his work with the Nebraska deer season. We three reminisced about the delicate round glass ornaments, decorated with stripes of silver, red, and green, and how upsetting it was when one fell to the hardwood floor, shattering. We also recalled the painstaking task of hanging the individual strands of shiny tinsel and our obsession with hanging them straight. We told about seeing the tree for the first time in daylight on Christmas morning and the agony of having to wait to open presents until after breakfast. The others listened with interest to our stories. For Mindy and my niece and nephew, most of the stories were new.

I had prepared an activity for the eleven of us. Among the folds of a cloth napkin on a wooden tray, I had arranged twenty-four ornaments. There was a fanciful dancing reindeer wearing a string of tiny colored lights; a crude, hand-cut tin star; a wooden snowflake; a brightly painted manger scene; a fat, resin snowman; a bread-dough Santa; and eighteen others. Each person got to pick one; for the next few days it could hang on my tree. The tray was passed around the family circle once, giving each person time to handle and examine all the ornaments. I shared back-stories about a few of them while we ate dessert from Mom's poinsettia plates.

After the tray's first round, it was time for our selections. I asked each person to tell the *why* behind their choice. Lois, as the oldest sibling, went first. She decided on a realistic chickadee perched on a sprig of bright berries. The tree in her own home featured snowflake decorations. I had included several of those but she explained she wanted something bright and reminiscent of Daddy for this special ornament. I passed a small silver tray her way. On it were the tiniest of white tags, each with a loop of dark thread. Hers read,

"To Lois from Jean, 2003." After fastening it to the chickadee, she hung the colorful bird on the tree while the next person examined the tray a second time. Thus it went, each person making a selection and telling us something about the choice. The crude metal star, purchased in the Amish country of Pennsylvania, reminded Lois's husband of something his grandfather would have made. My nephew has a Santa collection, so claiming one of the Santa ornaments was a natural for him. When it was Mindy and Samuel's turn, I assumed Mindy would pick one for her six-month-old son. Not so. To my delight, she leaned him over the tray. He studied the items carefully. His eyes and hand fell upon a bright red sequined butterfly. I hung it on the tree for him.

The next day we experienced our long-anticipated Christmas. Mindy and my niece and nephew were touched when they opened the *Grandpa's Greatest Memories* books. Before Lois and Robert opened their photo albums, I encouraged everyone to move to where they could see Daddy's last pictures. As each page was turned, I explained what I knew about the photograph. After several pages my eyes filled with tears and my voice began to catch; within seconds, my daughter instinctively was placing Samuel Levi on my lap. He looked quietly into my eyes. After kissing his soft, sweet-smelling forehead, I was able to continue.

As the gift opening progressed, there were reminders at every turn of Daddy, and of Mother, too. Sentiment lay close to the surface. We had wished fervently Daddy would have been alive to share this Christmas. However, rather than being sad, we truly were enjoying the time together, as evidenced by the excited chatter.

"Ted! The pot's empty. Can you make some more coffee?" Robert asked from the kitchen.

"Sure. I'll get right on it." Several people had agreed to assume jobs to help the day's activities move along. Ted, the major coffee aficionado in the group, was tasked with keeping coffee available in my small Mr. Coffee coffee-maker.

So it went. Snacking. Conversing. Laughing. Watching each other open gifts, one at a time, gifts that were not expensive but given from the heart.

It was my turn to open another gift. Gold paper with a cream-colored snowflake pattern on the package from my sister and her husband caught my eye. "This is beautiful paper, Lois."

"It's been saved for several years now. That was from Mother's collection of Christmas paper." We exchanged smiles.

Throughout the couple of hours of gift-opening, we grazed on chips, pistachios, peanut brittle, and Christmas candy. I had included treats traditional in our family, including caramels and ribbon candy "Santa Daddy" had always supplied.

"What's the music that's playing?" asked my niece. "I love the mix of Christmas songs!"

"It's a CD Mindy gave me. Interestingly enough…as a Hanukkah present. Let me grab the CD case and I'll tell you exactly."

"No need. I just wondered if it was a radio station."

I stooped to help Samuel turn the crank on his new jack-in-the-box. His arms flew up with surprise each time the clown popped out.

As I turned around, I observed that a narrow ray of sunlight had made its way through the front window and across two rooms, somehow failing to be blocked by intervening objects or people. It had achieved its goal: to spotlight new pink blossoms on the African violet that originally had been my mom's. One more unexpected gift.

With everyone's help, the early evening dinner came together. Lois read the blessing Daddy had composed years ago for another family dinner. Samuel was patient with us all. A friend had described him as polite, an unusual term for a six-month-old. However, he was indeed polite with us, enabling us to take pleasure in the extended dinner and conversation, as well as his calm but happy presence.

When I brought the dessert tray to the table, Lois was the first to note the non-traditional addition. There, among the myriad of fruit breads, sweets, and fancy cookies, I had placed that favorite of Daddy's: Fig Newtons.

All too soon, Christmas Day was over. After everyone dispersed for the night, I sat quietly in the darkened living room, basking in the light from the tree and attempting to embed the happenings of the day deeply, permanently in my memory.

From whatever constituted *the owl*...from wherever resided its essence...I sensed approval.

The remaining two days passed too quickly. The holiday event had arrived like an ocean wave, swelling magnificently, creating a vivid experience, and receding, carrying with it much of what had been. My hosting of the holiday fell short of my perfectionist expectations, yet I had done what I could. I sincerely hoped our Christmas time had supplied each family member with a reserve of memories on which to reflect in the days and years to come.

New Year's Eve 1999

Four years earlier I celebrated New Year's Eve with my father. I had known for many years that if he were still alive, and if it were at all feasible, I would be with him when 1999 became 2000. As long as I can remember, my father had talked about wanting to see the year 2000. Many people probably had the same desire, but few made such a big deal of it as did my dad.

So, early in 1999 during one of our Sunday evening phone calls, I asked, "How would it be if I came out to celebrate New Year's Eve with you this year?"

"That would be wonderful," he said. "I always wanted to live to see the year 2000. It would be fun to celebrate together." From then on, we talked about it often.

That December I purchased party hats and paper horns, glow-in-the-dark eyeglass frames that outlined the year 2000, and a big teddy bear for Daddy with "LOVE" embossed on one big foot and "2000" on the other. I bought "2000" champagne glasses so we could toast the new year. I also added a ratchety-sounding wooden noisemaker to our celebration collection.

I arrived the afternoon of December 30th. Early in our time together I asked, "When should we have our New Year's celebration?"

He thought for a couple of seconds. "I kind of thought it should be at midnight, if that's OK with you."

"Great! That's what I was hoping. Celebrating at any other time wouldn't have the same excitement."

I was thrilled. I had hoped we would be witnessing the actual change from 1999 to 2000, but I had been prepared for the fact my father might not feel up to it. With our decision made as to the timing of our celebration, we had the remainder of that evening and the next day to make final preparations. I suggested we plan to dress up for this momentous occasion; I encouraged him to wear his best suit. He good-naturedly agreed. In anticipation of the event, I had brought along a sequined top, long black skirt, and sassy shoes.

We planned to wear our dressy attire to the Hillcrest residents' New Year's Eve party. It was scheduled for three in the afternoon on the 31st. At first, I was surprised at the mid-afternoon time for the New Year's festivities, but I should not have been. By eight most evenings, the building is quiet and the halls deserted except for my dad and sometimes one other resident at the jigsaw-puzzle table.

When we entered the upstairs party room, his fellow residents smiled and exclaimed over our fancy clothes. Only one other person was wearing something other than everyday clothes. My dad's willingness to dress up was another example of how his enthusiasm for life benefitted others.

After the afternoon party and an early dinner, we walked across the parking lot to the care center to visit Mom, taking party hats for her and for her beloved teddy bear. Mother had regressed so far into the world of dementia she had no awareness of the time of day, much less the month or year. Nonetheless, she looked at us more carefully than usual, her eyes slowly taking in our cone-shaped hats and dressy clothes. She even reached over to touch my sparkly sequins. She allowed us to put a party hat on her; we dressed teddy in his also. Although Mom no longer spoke, whatever cells were functioning in her brain generated a rare smile for us that evening.

Back at his apartment, Daddy took a nap in his recliner while I prepared for our party. After he was awake, we watched TV as we munched on cookies, peanut brittle, and apple slices. The New

Year's celebrations around the world were varied, but all were spectacularly flamboyant. At midnight, we toasted each other with our flutes of bubbly beverages, blew our party horns, and twirled the rackety-sounding noisemaker. (We wondered the next day if we had awakened anyone.) A few minutes after midnight, we walked the deserted hallway to the front desk, where night-deskman Joe obligingly took our picture with the wall clock reading twelve-o-eight in the background. One of my dad's long-held dreams had come true. That evening is one of my favorite memories… an event that can never be duplicated.

Beginning Another New Year

Another New Year's Eve was almost here. I had a date with a handsome, dark-eyed fellow, younger and energetic, who appeared to be quite interested in me. I was excited to be with Samuel Levi on his first New Year's Eve.

I did not wear my sequined top this New Year's Eve. But I did go into my grandson's room at midnight. As he slept in his crib, I leaned over, placed my hand lightly on his shoulder, and whispered, "Happy New Year, Samuel." To my surprise, he awoke and smiled at me. As quickly as he had awakened, he went back to sleep; soon I, too, was slumbering peacefully under a warm blanket on the living room sofa. Invisibly draped atop that soft covering was the patchwork quilt of my life, to which had been added a few more lovely stitches.

Thus began the new year. Each day brought an additional minute or two of daylight. In contrast to the winter solstice sun setting before 4:30, it was now after 4:40 by the time the sun slipped below the horizon. Even considering January's bitter cold, having a few more minutes of daylight was welcome.

On the evening of the seventh of January, I reluctantly determined it was time to remove the decorations from my Christmas tree. I had anticipated this enhanced holiday for thirteen months. Therefore, it was not easy to let go of its last physical remnants.

I put on my new Christmas CD, the one we had listened to on Christmas Day, when I had it on repeat play. I worked steadily as I listened. As always I was amazed at the speed of the *undecorating* in contrast to the *decorating* of the tree. In less than an hour, I had singlehandedly removed and packed away everything, including the lights.

One of the last ornaments I removed from the tree was the glass owl. It had spent the holidays watching over our festivities. I had felt its reassuring presence. Now, nestled among my other holiday treasures, the ornamental owl would hibernate until the next December.

After the decorations were put away, I sat in the presence of the barren fir that had given its life to be a Christmas tree. I was shelling pistachios. The taste of the slightly salty, green-tinged nuts was satisfying. The powerful "Alleluia Chorus" of Handel's *Messiah* began. I knew it was the last track of the CD. This time, it was not set on replay. I consumed a few more nuts as the final triumphant strains played out.

The house fell quiet…except for the ever-present tick-tock of the wall clock. I ceremoniously lit the ivory-colored pillar candle on the dining room table. Nestled in a footed dish that had belonged to my mother, it had burned many hours during the holidays. The top inch and a half was glowing again. Although the holidays were past, the sentiment, memories, and a few physical reminders remained.

The tree would be recycled. I would vacuum the crunchy needles from the living room floor, sweep the front porch of the tree's leavings, and rearrange the furniture. Step by purposeful step, the long-anticipated holiday was destined to move further into the past. I sat pensively in the flickering candlelight…feeling…remembering.

Canada Geese

On my route to work I drive past several areas of open space, parks and other expanses of groomed grass, now brown and dormant, periodically buried under a mantle of white. A highlight of my morning drive is spotting the Canada geese that frequent this part of the city and graze in these verdant areas.

Yesterday's Arctic cold front brought sub-zero nighttime temperatures. As I started my drive, I was wishing I had worn gloves to handle the icy-cold steering wheel. After a mile and a half I began to watch for geese. They have favorite morning feeding spots, and I usually see scores of the magnificent birds in at least one of those areas. The first sweeping expanse of grass was vacant. Further on, in a protected area where I seldom see them, were about a dozen. Their nearby acre of lake was frozen solid; often, I see them swimming in the thirty-some degree water on mornings when the air temperature is well below freezing. I mentally sifted through plans for the day, dealt with traffic issues, and curled my fingers into fists against the cold. So, where were the others? Perhaps in the park with the ancient willow. If that were the case, I wouldn't see them. Ahead on the crest of the hill lay a wide median separating the two northbound lanes from those heading south. There were the geese, perhaps fifty of them, crowding onto the grassy median. They had responded instinctively to the dynamics of temperature and airflow. The coldest air had sought the lower pockets of the landscape. The asphalt roads, warmed somewhat by the earliest rays of the winter sun, lay on either side of their higher haven. Food and a warmer domain had drawn them there. They spilled out onto one lane of oncoming traffic. It was the direction less traveled at this time of day; nonetheless, it was a dangerous situation for them. Vehicles slowed as they approached and the flock made room for their fellow stragglers on the traffic island. I took it all in within a couple of seconds as I drove by.

Instinct. Survival. This morning the Canada geese demonstrated both. I believe we humans also possess the instinct for survival. This morning the geese were being drawn to a different place. The same seemed to be happening to me. But to where?

The Nightmare

Throughout January, uplifting times such as watching for the geese were counterbalanced by emotionally challenging episodes. One night began with the uncommon-for-me ordeal of lying awake several hours, unable to fall asleep. With eventual sleep came the dream. No, it was not a dream. It was a nightmare. In one respect, it was not related to the death of my father. On the other hand, the nightmare probably was a reflection of the loss of control in my life.

It was one of those dreams that seemed to last most of the night. In the dream, I was struggling emotionally. I had gone to the home of my college boyfriend, who represented someone I thought I could rely on for support and empathy. When he opened the door, I stepped inside and started to give him a casual hug. He refused it. It was clear he was no longer available to me as a friend. In my dream, the awkwardness of the situation, coupled with hurtful, unexpected rejection, had a disproportionately devastating effect on me. Desperate to escape the anxiety-producing experience, I ran into another room of his house and crawled out a window. From there, I dove into deep, dark waters, spending an eternity submerged in suffocating confusion. My desperate efforts to find a place of emotional and physical safety were thwarted at every turn. Eventually I found myself deposited on a beach, gasping for breath. But rather than having reached a place of refuge, I watched in terror as gigantic waves destroyed the protective sea wall. Next, the powerful surge of ocean waters swept away a bridge offering my sole means of escape. Amidst the chaos of the devastation, I felt petrified, isolated, and totally helpless.

I awoke with a start...tense and emotionally drained. I opened one eye to see if daylight had arrived. The answer was no. As I closed my eye, the lid squeezed out a single tear. It slowly inched its way sideways across the bridge of my nose. One teardrop, the only physical evidence of my nightmare trauma. I crawled out of bed and found my way through the darkness to the bathroom, where I drank a large glass of cool water. That helped. I went back to bed, still burdened by an unshakable anxiety and a profound melancholy.

Before I knew it, my alarm clock sounded. In the interim between going back to sleep and being awakened by the alarm, I had relaxed and slept well. I felt driven to renew my *search for the owl*. Suddenly I stopped. What if our roles had reversed earlier that morning? Perhaps it had been *the owl* that had found *me* and guided me to that blessed drink of cool water.

Challenge of Winter

If early human beings had lived in the climate I was experiencing, where frigid days and long winter nights prevailed, would they have hibernated? Wouldn't it be preferable to straining against the inhospitable natural environment and long hours of darkness? My soul wanted to hibernate...or, at least for a while, to hide away. Commitments of many kinds and a modern lifestyle made that impractical, if not impossible.

During this cold, dark wintertime, I was continually challenged; the loss of my father weighed heavily on me. Sundays were especially difficult. I missed those casual but loving phone conversations.

Mid-morning I headed to the grocery store to purchase one of my favorite orange cinnamon rolls to have with a leisurely, late breakfast. On my way, the road passed over a small brook edged in lacy ice. Although I couldn't stop for a closer look, even a glimpse of nature's artistry was gratifying.

At the store I discovered they were sold out of cinnamon rolls. The child in me was crushed. As often had been the case throughout the several months of my grieving, a seemingly small happening or memory had the power to overwhelm. The frustrated adult in me selected a different pastry and carried it home. The grieving child carried home the disappointment.

Back home, I inched up the thermostat four degrees from its nighttime setting. I brewed a pot of strong coffee, the last of the Starbucks Christmas Blend my brother-in-law had supplied at the holidays. The blinds were open but the interior of my home was still gloomy; the sky outside was grey and solemn. Again, I lit the pillar candle on the dining room table. It shed a soft light; the flame burned steady and tall. The phenomena of the physical world do not discern emotion: the candle burned the same today in the presence of my disappointment and heavy heart as it did that festivity-filled Christmas day.

The next day would have been Mother's birthday. Hers came shortly before Dad's, so in recent years I would have been planning a trip to celebrate his. The automatic emotional anticipation of another trip welled up within me, only to be doused by the remembrance Daddy was dead. I knew I would honor his special day in my own way; but for now, the idea of the day without him brought new depths to my despondency. I struggled to find the optimism and strength that usually sustained me, yet intellectually, I knew this phase of my grieving would not last.

January Reflections

A few days later I took time to record more of my observations and reflections.

> A skiff of snow blankets the earth again this morning, but the sun is bright and the sky, a pale blue. Looking out at the roof of the garage, I note the rectangular outlines of the shingles and a sketch of the shadow of a tree, drawn across the roof by the low-lying winter sun. Nature's patterns, rhythms, and wise ways rejuvenate me whenever I take the time to notice them.
>
> The winter days of late have vacillated between harshness and kindness to us human beings. Cycles of approximately five days bring cold and snow followed by a respite, such as today when the sun will feel warm as I drive to work, and snow in

sunlit areas will melt. With sundown will come an immediate plunge in temperature.

The sidewalk beside my home lies continuously in shadow at this time of year. Its patches of black ice worry me, especially as I traverse them after dark. As I gingerly cross the sloping, icy areas, I sense what my father in his last few years must have experienced: concern about falling. He was a dignified gentleman who carried himself with poise as well as humility. His awareness of the potentially life-altering results of a fall was obvious when we walked with him. He had begun carrying a cane, even though in most situations he did not use it as an aid to walking. He more frequently transformed it into a handy pointer. When he truly didn't need it, the cane often was left behind, forcing him to retrace his steps to find it. We laughed whenever that happened. But carrying the cane was insurance-in-hand. He wasn't fearful, just sensible. And appropriately cautious.

That attitude prevailed in the manner in which he lived his life. He lived optimistically in the present and didn't allow himself to be consumed by worry. My search for the owl is helping me analyze, appreciate, and work at developing those complementary traits of optimism and appropriate preparedness.

Reminders of Dad

For several months I have started and ended each day with thoughts of my dad: it has been inevitable, for on my nightstand are happy reminders. When I silence my alarm each morning, I am greeted by sunlight filtering through the slits of my bedroom blinds, causing the bubbles inside a clear glass paperweight to sparkle. I had given the three-inch orb to my dad. It reminded me of Henry David Thoreau's detailed description of air bubbles in the ice he observed at his beloved Walden Pond. Ten years ago, I had sent my dad a copy of *Walden*, purchased on my trip to Massachusetts when I visited Walden Pond. The paperweight gift had followed with a note about the ice. Now mine, it continues to be a reminder of our shared admiration for Thoreau.

When I retire for the night, the last light on is the one beside my bed. When I switch off the lamp, I am sometimes surprised by, but mostly have come to anticipate, the joyful glow-in-the-dark plastic eyeglasses that read, *2000*. When I brought them here from Daddy's apartment in April, I casually set them on my nightstand. Temporarily, I thought. But when I learned they would be the last thing I saw before falling asleep, I chose to leave them there. Following our millennium celebration, Daddy perched them on the face of his big teddy bear; the bear sat propped against a pillow on his double bed. The glasses also had been worn for a humorous three-generation photograph of my dad, brother, and nephew. My dad had valued them enough to keep them on continual display, so I was doing the same.

After an overnight temperature near zero, the sun was warming the earth and reflecting brightly off yesterday's three inches of new snow. I checked the outside thermometer. It was already twenty-five degrees. I had slept in, but was eager to begin a non-structured day when I could catch up on whatever I chose, with none of my *real* jobs demanding my time.

The next day was my dad's birthday. I thought ahead to the not-too-far-away date in early spring, the first anniversary of his death. A wave of queasiness and uncertainty swept over me; I felt lightheaded and panicky. What power our thoughts have over our physical responses. Fortunately, I was aware my way of thinking was creating my emotional funk. I knew Daddy would not want me to feel this way. A smile or even a laugh associated with memories of the fun we shared would be more what he'd have wanted for me.

I quit thinking of him dying and of the suffering he endured on the last day of his life. I turned to the joyful memories of one year ago today, when I had arrived on the eve of his birthday in anticipation of our time together. These memories were certain to nurture and sustain me: those of loving and being loved.

My Father's Birthday

My alarm sounded at 5:30 a.m. I turned on the bedside lamp. Within seconds the thought of my early morning commitment catapulted me out of bed. For once I took no note of the bubble-filled glass globe. I needed to be at Mindy's by 6:40 to care for Samuel Levi.

The crisp air filled my nostrils as I stepped out the front door. It had been another frigid night. The sky was aglow with a pink and blue watercolor wash on this, the dawn of February 13th. What had the weather been on the barren plains of western Nebraska on the day my dad was born, ninety-five years ago? Was it warm inside the small sod house?

I trudged through two-day-old snow to my garage. To the south, a bright quarter-moon hung low, more than halfway through its arc in the winter sky. Neither new nor full. Neither rising nor setting. Did this portend something? Was it a reminder of my unfinished quest?

I began the fifteen-minute drive to my daughter's to be with Samuel for a couple of hours before taking him to daycare and going to work. Beneath the pastel sky, the stark white of the snow-clad mountains to the west glowed in the first light of day. A valley of twinkling lights lay in between. I felt a sense of adventure in the early morning hour, similar to when I was leaving before dawn on a long car trip to see my dad.

Early morning one year ago, I was driving from my motel to eat breakfast with Daddy. I thought back to our cheerful greeting when he opened his apartment door on the birthday that turned out to be his last. I recalled the colorful balloon he had taken with him to breakfast, the combination birthday/Valentine celebration, and the leisurely dinner Daddy and I had enjoyed that evening.

The stoplight blinked green and brought me back to the present. I headed on toward my daughter's. It was growing lighter; however, it was early enough on this frigid morning that the Canada geese were not yet in evidence. Where had they spent the long winter night?

My daughter and I exchanged greetings and custody of Samuel, then she hastily departed. Adam was on a business trip which was why I needed to take care of Samuel. Mindy had to be at work before the daycare opened, and Adam usually did not.

Now seven and one half months old, Samuel was accustomed to busying himself with serious play for long periods of time, yet he paused long enough to flash a smile my way as I came into the room. I appreciated the opportunity to share some time with Samuel Levi, my dad's descendant and namesake, on the anniversary of Dad's birth. As Samuel played, I sat on the floor nearby.

We both saw it: the quick flash of movement beyond the patio door was enough to turn our heads and capture our attention. A sparrow had braved the six-degree morning to greet us. It explored the tiny hanging birdhouse, swaying with its sudden weight. We watched it intently. In the wink of an eye, the bird was gone.

All too soon it was time for us to leave. I swaddled him in his thick one-piece fleece coverall and secured him in the car seat. As I headed the car toward the daycare center, he began to cry. Even bundled as he was, the little being was cold. So I sang, over and over, "Samuel Levi, Samuel Levi," as I had done many times in the several months of his young life. Immediately quieted, he listened to the varied rhythms of my made-up tune. Within eight minutes we were there. As I carried him from the car to the entry, I was more careful about keeping him warm. It felt wonderful holding him against me.

I found his care providers and gave each of them a valentine from Samuel. The cards were a day early because this year, Valentine's Day fell on a Saturday. They fussed appropriately over his new red corduroy shirt, chosen by his mom for the holiday. He eagerly began playing a small plastic piano. I smiled as I left, reflecting on his flexibility.

Several years ago when my mom and dad were still alive, I had baked and frosted heart-shaped sugar cookies and mailed them along with a sentimental card and letter as my Valentine's Day gift. When they received them, my dad had left a telephone message for me expressing his sincere appreciation for the values I referred to in my letter and for the gift of my baking.

The memory planted a seed in my mind that was growing into a plan. Next year on this date, it again would be the anniversary of my dad's birth and Valentine's eve. I anticipated making, baking, and decorating heart-shaped cookies with Samuel. They could be a surprise Valentine gift from him to his mom and dad. Samuel would be nineteen months old next year at this time. His spreading of the frosting, to say nothing of the probable tasting, could create not only a Kodak moment, but the beginning of what I hoped would become a tradition.

After arriving at work, I checked my messages. I had a call from a fellow whom Daddy and I had met a few years ago when we were in Grand Lake. He and my dad had exchanged letters from time to time; he valued the historical information Dad could provide about Grand Lake Lodge. When I had a chance, I returned his call. Ironically, he had been thinking of my dad, so he called to inquire about him. I apologized for not informing him of my dad's death. Yet it was a joy for me, on today of all days, to hear him reflect on my father's keen mind, excellent writing skills, and vivid memory. We chatted for several minutes. I promised to keep in touch.

The day I originally had anticipated with apprehension continued to unfold in a comfortable fashion. I found caring listeners whenever I was moved to mention my dad. As the day progressed, I heard myself explaining how sadness and memories of my dad's zest for life were incompatible. Every time I said it, I became more convinced of its truth. I found myself experiencing his birthday with genuine joy.

Valentine's Day

For the past few years I'd celebrated Valentine's Day with my dad due to its proximity to his birthday. I remembered last year's turkey-watching and the turquoise-colored stone he purchased for me. It is indeed a treasure, kept in a purple suede pouch that is part of an elaborately beaded Native American necklace.

This year I knew I'd need to reinvent Valentine's Day. Although I no longer had my father, this year...for the first time...I had a grandson in my life. I had purchased two valentines: one for Samuel and one for Mindy and Adam. The one I selected for Samuel featured a perky black-and-white puppy. Its fur spots were heart-shaped. Inside Mindy and Adam's valentine I wrote a lengthy note about their qualities as parents and the strong sense of family they were creating.

I had arranged to deliver the cards early in the afternoon. Adam had returned from his business trip the night before and was at home with Mindy. Samuel was napping when I arrived. A few minutes later, hearing Samuel was awake, I offered to get him up. I slowly opened the door to his bedroom. He flashed a big smile when he saw me. I lifted his solid body into my arms. As we crossed the room, he turned back toward his crib; he wanted something there. I retraced my steps and leaned him over the bed. He stuck out his right hand and retrieved a favorite toy, carrying it proudly to the living room. I thanked him for the valentine I had received in the mail at my home. The return address had read, "Sam Cohen." How grown-up that sounded. I commented to Mindy about handwriting style being hereditary, because although it was his name, the writing on the envelope had looked like hers. She smiled, acknowledging my attempt at humor.

Samuel sat on my lap while he opened his valentine. He was especially attracted to the shiny red foil stickers on the envelope. He scratched at them with his fingernails, trying to lift them off the paper. I explained to him that hearts are symbols of love, and I loved him a lot. He probably didn't comprehend my words, but I believe he felt my love.

That evening I went out for a Valentine's Day dinner with a friend. (I hadn't worn my little black dress since my dad's birthday dinner 366 days earlier!) Easy conversation and a pampering environment contributed to an enjoyable, rare night out.

It had been a heartfelt Valentine's Day, another reassuring reminder of how pleasant life still could be, even without my dad.

Returning to the Park

The sky was overcast, an enormous inverted dome of mottled grey marble. The thermometer read almost sixty, but when the light breeze blew, it carried with it a hint of cold from the softening snow banks. Even so, it was a good day to return to the park. My last visit had been three months before. I was surprised it had been so long.

Once at the park, I headed north on foot, following the asphalt path past the play area. After several hundred steps I detoured to visit the pond. On its steel blue surface swam two dozen ducks plus a few Canada geese. A few others sat on the twenty-foot-wide band of ice at the pond's shaded south end. Pairs of mallard ducks were behaving in their own male-female way: they bobbed their heads rhythmically at each other, and the drake mounted the female in a splashy connection. True to their nature as well as their name, several others repeatedly ducked into the water to search for food. Some in shallow water fed half-hidden, with their tail feathers pointing skyward. Others stayed submerged fifteen to twenty seconds, reappearing at the surface within ten feet of where they had disappeared.

I walked far beyond the pond to my ultimate destination: a hilltop gazebo with a square concrete table and benches overlooking the valley. Nearby were several ponderosa pines, a few spruce trees, and a proliferation of tall, wild grasses. Clumps of rabbitbrush were heavy with amber crowns of last fall's seeds. I welcomed the distant view of the valley and the mountains beyond, as well as the company of the adjacent trees and undergrowth. I sat facing the valley and mountains, my back to the sun as well as the breeze. I had come prepared to do some writing. I scribbled a few sentences. Already the breeze felt chilly. I adjusted the hood of my jacket to cover my neck and hair, but it didn't help. What had been a breeze minutes earlier transformed into a wind. It was getting colder; I was not dressed for this hilltop location. I was disappointed. Reluctantly I retraced my steps.

As I made my way with long steady strides back along the walkway, I heard an unfamiliar rattling sound overhead. I craned my neck and spotted scores of curlicue locust pods high in the tree, chattering to me via the stiff wind. I collected a well-curled specimen from the grass at the edge of the path. I stroked its velvety surface and noted its rich umber hue. I shook it to hear the rattling of its many flat, dry seeds.

Overhead, the seedpods continued to shiver in the wind, demanding I pay attention. Their urgent message seemed to be, "Remember!" And I did. I remembered wind-downed locust pods had been abundant last April. They were among the souvenirs of nature I had collected prior to my father's services, now more than ten months ago. I had been enamored with them. Now, here they were again, evidence of the completion of yet another of nature's cycles.

A line of Canada geese sketched the sky overhead. I counted one, two, three…up to nine. I marveled at the smooth course of their plump bodies through the air, while their wings moved in wide, smooth swaths above and below the unwavering line of their flight.

Once back inside my vehicle, protected from the cold wind, I sat in quiet reflection. My disappointment at not having had the opportunity to write had been countered by the flyover of the geese and my discovery of the locust pods. Indeed, the very wind that had kept me from writing had made possible the seedpod communication. It was an excellent life lesson about not reacting too quickly, but accepting what *is*; I had acquired a bit more of the wisdom of the owl.

Almost Spring

The varied weather of late February served as a harbinger of spring. One morning a fluffy, wet snow created not outlines of my garage-roof shingles, but a puffy pattern of hundreds of miniature white pillows. Two days later, bird songs heralded the warming morning. I heard one of my favorites, the chickadee, auditioning for the spring program with its two-note call.

By noon I noted even though clouds outnumbered the patches of blue sky, narrow rivulets of melting snow were streaking the otherwise dry sidewalks and roads. Enough moisture had fallen in recent days for the birdbath on my patio to be nearly full of water. Now liquid, this morning the contents had been an icy disc.

That afternoon I received a phone call from a friend who, also having recently lost a person dear to her, had known how to be wonderfully supportive at the time of my dad's death. She, too, had been watching the signs of approaching spring. My story of having experienced the milestone of my father's birthday led to a conversation about how cherishing memories honors the loved one. She agreed that not until death takes away the possibility of sharing a physical presence with someone do we fully understand the unique qualities of that person. Thus it has been with me and my remembrance of my dad.

Yes, death was teaching me many lessons. In addition to the value I found in memories of my dad, death also was teaching me to cherish my own days. The inevitability of death was an urgent reminder to live in such a manner I might leave a legacy of creative energy, a youthful spirit, and devotion to the natural world. Death encouraged me to tell my stories, stories not only of how it *was*, but of how it *is* with me. And I must celebrate the wonders of nature as they continue to appear. After all, are not these almost-spring happenings an essential part of the cycle of life and death?

Late Afternoon with Samuel

The winter weather was mild the Wednesday I picked up Samuel from his daycare. He was sitting on the carpet playing with toys when I stepped into the room. When he saw me, his mouth, eyes, eyebrows, and double chin all smiled. He forgot his playthings and reached out to me. My heart was like soft butter, melting. I gathered him into my arms, hugging his aliveness against my body.

Samuel's new daycare was in a private home two blocks from his house. I had parked my car, picked up his stroller, and walked over to get him so the two of us could enjoy the outdoors and take our time going home. Along the way we passed a pine tree overhanging the street; its low braches encroached upon the sidewalk and hung at the level of Samuel's stroller. We stopped to explore the conveniently located branch. With focused curiosity, he touched the long needles as I talked to him about them being sharp and stiff. I pointed out the quarter-inch reddish cone developing within the whorl of needles at the tip of one branch.

Within minutes we arrived at the house. I paused at the driveway; his mom's roses would be blooming before long. At the same time, I was remembering that someone else was now tending what had been my dad's beloved front-yard rosebushes. I unbuckled the belt on Samuel's stroller and lifted him into my arms. I let him finger the brightly painted house sign above the doorbell, a plaque Mindy had created soon after they purchased their home.

For the next two hours we played, read books, fingered some keys on the piano and sang, and played some more. He giggled when I made the spotted cloth giraffe-toy pop out of its cone-shaped hiding place. I had brought the toy to the hospital on the day he was born.

Samuel's vocal experiments were frequent. What an experience it must be for a little one to realize they possess the ability to produce varied sounds at will. Throughout the afternoon, Samuel sputtered as he blew bubbles, repeated his favorite letter sound "d-d-d-d-d," and rubbed his rattle against his mouth as he vocalized, creating humorous undulating noises.

Afternoon eased into early evening. Mindy and Adam had arrived home; it was time for me to depart. After hugs and kisses, I stepped outside into the cool night air.

I had parked my vehicle on the street in front of their house. Before driving away, I glanced at their picture window. There stood Adam, holding Samuel so he could watch me leave. He waved Samuel's small hand. I waved back. Samuel's little hand kept waving good-bye. As I inched my car forward, he continued to wave for as long as I could see him at the window.

Waving good-bye. Watching a loved one leave. Honoring the connection even as the physical proximity is diminishing. So it always has been with me and those I love. Waving in the dark… waving from an airplane window even when no one could see me… waving good-bye…

Good-bye / Hello

Waving good-bye. Saying hello. These are among the transitions inherent in the flow of our lives. While harboring pleasant memories of Samuel's recent good-bye waves, I was moved to write about *hellos*:

> On these almost-spring days, although nighttime minutes still outnumber those of day, the sun says hello with brilliant morning rays streaming over the horizon or, in the case of the view from my townhome, over the rooflines to the east. The light of the sun greets the last tired snow banks that have retreated into the diminishing shade. They are as pleased with the warm welcome as I was a few days ago with Samuel's; they, too, melt.
>
> Although overnight temperatures still regularly dip below freezing, spring is not far away. The buds on the aspen trees near my doorstep are swollen but have yet to reveal their long catkins.

Amidst the dry, raffia-colored blades of last year's lawn have emerged thin sprouts of green, nurtured by the moisture from each snowfall, but longing for the gentle touch of rain.

I, too, experience the sun's hello each morning. The glass globe sparkles more enthusiastically in the increasingly direct sunlight. I, too, am invigorated, ready for new growth. Yet an undeniable dichotomy conflicts my being: the pleasant sense of anticipation of spring is positioned opposite my reluctance to experience the painful memories of that time of year. Why was it in the season of eternal hope and promise, that my dad died? The questions tug at my soul. Why then? Why, in the season my dad felt especially excited about being alive, was it his time to die? I cry softly, wishing for an answer, yet knowing there is no answer other than the reminder that what transpired is real; it did happen.

I have ceased being concerned about my tears. Instead, they serve to honor my beloved father and to reassure me of the depth of my love for him. They remind me also of how dearly I was loved. I cry more as I experience the crux of opposites, of loss and of love. My sobs touch the walls and fill the world of my home. I blow my nose and dry my tearful eyes. I know I am preparing myself for the arrival of spring and the anniversary of my dad's death.

> Where is the owl? Is it here? If it is, it is silent, but this morning its essence seems to be flowing into me, filling the void created by the spent tears. Do I still need to go in search of the owl? Lately the owl has been finding me and guiding me toward those lessons I needed to learn on my own.

As I finished writing, the two-note call of a chickadee sounded from afar. Hearing it, I pictured the paper maché chickadee perched on the shelf at my daughter's home; she had sent it with me last year to watch over my dad in his final days. Perhaps the chickadee had called to him late that Thursday afternoon, offering its loving energy as he left life behind.

PART FIVE

The Second Spring

First Day of Spring

The new season officially arrived last evening after I turned in for the night. Over the last few days, I had devised a plan for today, the day that began the *second* spring without my dad. I set my alarm for an earlier-than-usual hour so I had time for a leisurely morning: before heading for work I would visit my friend the willow.

A maintenance worker for the park, finished with his chores, was backing his vehicle out as I arrived. I flagged him down to thank him for the role he played in caring for this urban oasis, a place of importance to me and many others. Surprised and pleased, he thanked me, also. Insulated coffee mug in hand, I made my way along the curving concrete sidewalk. The park was nearly deserted. In the distance two adults longingly eyed the playground but sauntered on.

The brisk air was refreshing. A bank of clouds to the east covered the rising sun; blue skies comprised the view to the west. This time there was no frost to impede my steps across the footbridge to my favourite vantage point, the observation platform. I slowed my pace as I approached the venerable willow, waiting solemnly for me.

Though an air of serenity pervaded the atmosphere, jubilant bird overtures greeted me in surround-sound. My eyes traced the lines of the pruned willow branches, interrupted by bud after swollen bud of pale green. I studied the earth below. A low-growing juniper bush was showing an intense blue-green. Perhaps it provided shelter for the cottontails I had observed here on previous visits. The dense growth of its evergreen mound easily could camouflage a rabbit burrow. Here and there, having conquered the hard-packed soil, the jagged leaves of dandelions had sprouted. Everything I observed carried the energy of this first day of spring.

With a flurry of wings and accompanying bird-chatter, four feisty flickers descended noisily to play in the arena of the giant willow. Flashing their bright, burnt-umber tail- and wing-feathers, they flitted from branch to branch. Was it a game of chase or an attempt at mating? With their cavorting and calling out to one another, the four feathered beings seemed to occupy more space than their small size would dictate. It was a flicker circus for two quick minutes, their movements so boisterous that to follow them with my eyes was nearly impossible. They jumped from trunk to branch to wispy twig escaping, cajoling, teasing, and wildly flailing their striped feathers. In a flurry of color and noise, they took off in unison to continue their antics elsewhere. Calm returned. Any apprehension over the arrival of the season of my dad's death had been replaced by reassuring feelings of joy and discovery.

My next stop was the grocery store where I bought two bunches of yellow daffodils. Their sunshine would brighten the gallery where I was to spend the day. My last stop was Kinko's. I had decided to celebrate the return of spring by once again distributing copies of "When It's Spring." I had ordered sixty bookmarks, printed on yellow cardstock, similar to those we had given out at Dad's services. I explained my project to the clerk as he rang up the sale. His glance went to the counter and fixed on the brightly colored stack. His eyes remained there. Seeing he was interested in reading the poem, I presented the first one to him and departed with the remaining fifty-nine.

I arrived early at the gallery. I cut half an inch off the daffodil stems and arranged the cheerful flowers in a vase. Their welcoming aura was perfect for the narrow table holding the guest book. I hung the windsock, put out the "OPEN" sign, and awaited the first visitors.

After a day of distributing bookmarks and interacting with customers, I arrived home tired but genuinely happy. I mustered enough energy to accomplish a few housekeeping tasks and turned in early. Before falling asleep, I lay quiet, thinking. Although I still missed my dad and thought of him often, the grief and panic of last spring were long gone.

Second Day of Spring

On its second day, the season again greeted me with a glorious morning burgeoning with energy. Outside my upstairs window, hanging from the tall aspen trees, furry catkins had appeared, similar to the poplar catkins observed in Dad's childhood and thus deserving of mention in his poem. The discovery was one more opportunity to note the synchronicity of my life and my dad's.

I left early for work. The traffic was light. A couple of miles into my drive, I reached the open areas where I often sighted Canada geese. I spotted more than a dozen. But this morning they had paired off, a noticeable deviation from their winter flocking behavior. Soon mating would be underway, eventually resulting in fuzzy goslings. I hoped Samuel Levi and I could seek out some of those baby geese on my birthday in May. As I drove past them, one sleek pair of geese became airborne off to my right. I immediately lost sight of them. Quickly they reappeared, reflected in my rear-view mirror. The two birds were flying five feet above the roadway, following me. My heart skipped a beat. They stayed on course with my vehicle, the dark eyes on their outstretched heads peering into my car. They continued behind me ten or more seconds, veered off to the right, and disappeared. I had been holding my breath. I allowed myself to breathe deeply as I savored the magical occurrence.

As I continued my *search for the owl*, I found myself thinking not only of my dad but, more and more, of my mother as well. Her dementia and death had led to the closeness Daddy and I developed during the last years of his life. But since Christmas, the remembrance of Daddy *and* Mother had been helping me better understand myself and my place in our family history. In my heart, the geese, this time as a couple, symbolized my parents. The geese reminded me of two additional things. First, the loving connection between two of the same species is what enables life to continue, and second, I was being watched over—sometimes literally—in more ways than I'd have guessed.

One of Mom's Treasures

My mother valued beautiful things: quality, aesthetically pleasing ones as opposed to anything lavish or expensive. And as did Daddy, she appreciated nature's beauty. Her colorful arrangements of flowers from our yard decorated our home throughout the growing season.

When Lois, Robert, and I were dividing Mom and Dad's things, our choices of what we each wanted to take home were surprisingly diverse. Neither Lois nor Robert expressed an interest in the green vase I equated with beauty and home. It had showcased many of the bouquets I remember from my youth. As far as I was concerned, it belonged filled with flowers and positioned beside a made-from-scratch birthday cake.

Yes, to me a vase was pale green, six inches tall, with an hourglass shape. This particular one appeared in several of my childhood drawings and paintings. Therefore when I was able to bring home something so full of memories, I considered myself to be ever so fortunate.

Its shape, allowing the lower portion of stems to fan out and tapering to collect them at their center-point, created appealing arrangements. Daffodils were particularly stunning in its classic shape and clear, green color. So one day in late March I selected this vase for my own daffodil bouquet. The sunshine yellow blossoms and the vase itself, with its positive connections, were nurturing to my still-indecisive spirit.

A Shift in Focus

I welcomed the fact that my reminiscing had broadened to include earlier years of our family history. I was appreciating those years more fully and becoming better at identifying their significant and memorable aspects.

The distance created by the passage of time since my father's death was shifting the focal length of my memory. Initially my grief and thoughts of him allowed me to be aware of little other than my loss. With time, more of the past had come into focus through the lens of that life-changing event. Similar to a camera lens, eventually the depth of field will allow everything to become clear to me. In the past few months, I had experienced an acceleration of the phenomenon.

It was a relief and a loss: a relief because there were countless other aspects of life to value and to learn from; a loss because concentrating my thoughts and energy on the memory of my father had become comforting and familiar. As I occupied myself less with those, I turned my attention outward to the ongoing business of living.

Six Days Left

On the heels of my revelation about the broadening perspective of my memory and the renewed awareness of the need to move forward with my life came a downturn in my outlook. Over the next few days, my spirit languished. Thoughts of the anniversary of my dad's death were unsettling. I had lost my customary positive nature. When I looked at myself in the mirror, the eyes looking back at me were as gaunt and empty as they were last April. Finally, when only six days remained before April third, I rediscovered myself.

I tried on various ideas about how I would spend the date I would forever connect with my father's death. Some ideas fit too tightly, confining me; some were too amorphous. Some situations I envisioned did not allow for me to experience the range of reactions I anticipated the day would bring forth. Although others had offered their company, my preference was to be alone. I needed to be able to process the experience on my own terms. I needed to be able to listen to myself and to be keenly aware of my surroundings. The *how* and *where* needed to be decided. I already had arranged to be away from work. I knew where I *would not* be. But where *would* I be?

Wherever it was, one thing was certain: the first year of my *search for the owl* would have drawn to a close.

Dichotomy Revisited

A few days later I welcomed the opportunity to spend a morning alone with young Samuel. Now nine months old, he busied himself with crawling and pulling himself up anywhere he could gain a handhold. He focused his attention for twenty minutes or more on exploring the aspects of a favorite toy.

In late morning, I put Samuel in his stroller and we went for a long walk. With the warm spring weather, birds were singing; therefore, the calm, sunny day had its own musical accompaniment. Yet wherever we ventured, an underlying theme was provided by the ever-present, woeful call of the mourning dove. The pairing of the joyful and the mournful was yet another example of the dichotomy defining my experience of spring. As delighted as I was in the discovery of each aspect of the season, the acknowledgment that Daddy was not alive to enjoy it lent a somber note to each situation.

Eventually Mindy was home and it was time for me to leave. It was the last time I would see Samuel before the rapidly approaching anniversary. As I departed I was struck by how quickly Samuel was growing and changing: without help, he began waving good-bye.

I was cognizant of the countdown. The anniversary was now three days away. It had taken a long time, but finally I had decided how and where I needed to spend the upcoming day. I was relieved to have made a decision and I was satisfied with my plan.

Ending All Over Again

Rain. A gentle, soaking rain had begun the night before, filling my shallow birdbath to overflowing. The overcast morning was refreshing: soft and cool. Delicate violet blossoms peeked out from amongst heart-shaped foliage in the large pot in view from my window. I was pleased that the violets, transplanted last year from outside Daddy's apartment, were thriving in my patio garden and their first-of-spring flowers had emerged today, the anniversary of his death.

I slipped into my faded jeans and a favorite sweater. I lifted Mother's long silver chain with its etched heart pendant over my head; the sterling heart hung close to my own. A breakfast of cereal and grapefruit would suffice. I wished I had been cutting along the spokes of the fruit membrane to serve breakfast to my dad. He loved fresh grapefruit. As I spooned out the bite-sized sections one by one, I noted I was removing them in counterclockwise order. I was performing a supposedly automatic action, differently. Yet another change.

The minute hand on the wall clock inched toward 8:40, time of the phone call I made a year ago, in keeping with my promise to call Lois sometime after 8:30. During that brief phone conversation, I learned of Daddy's early morning heart attack. He was in the last hours of his life. I had said my final good-bye to Daddy and had heard his voice for the last time. This year, rather than conversing with my dad, I busied myself collecting a few supplies for the day, including the black folding umbrella that had been his, and some dark-colored peeled crayons, paper, and masking tape: I wanted to create some gravestone rubbings. Yes, I had decided to drive to the cemetery where Mother and Daddy were buried.

As I was heading to the garage, I slipped on the wet pavement. My right knee hit the ground. The misstep resulted in a small tear in my jeans, but the skin was neither bleeding nor scraped, so all was well…except I would need to replace this pair of jeans. Today I would wear these with the scarcely noticeable new hole. I viewed the happening as part of being open to whatever the day would hold. Accepting this imperfection was but another example of my adaptation to change and commitment to move forward with my life.

I set off on my several-hour drive. The muted tones of the grey, rainy world were compatible with my quiet spirit. An intermittent wiper-speed was sufficient to sweep the droplets of moisture from the windshield. Soon I had left the urban environment and was surrounded by open fields; an occasional lone tree silhouetted itself in gracefully branching blackness against the silver sky. Between the roadway and the fields lay an endless strip of untended wildness. There, the tall remnants of last year's weed-grasses were burdened with moisture. Their rich golden colors reminded me of autumn. Within an hour of driving, the showers subsided. A gentle haze and thick cloud cover remained, creating an atmosphere more akin to the humid Midwest than to this part of the often-dry West.

I had no specific expectations for the day. I would follow my instincts and explore whatever presented itself, taking time wherever and whenever it seemed appropriate. I was hoping to see some birds as I drove. Potential perching places included fences, telephone wires, and road signs. Although they were few and far between on this cool, wet morning, I did spy lark buntings and western meadowlarks. The latter, their bright yellow breasts decorated with a handsome black *V*, were a welcome sign of spring. I left I-76 near Sterling to travel US-6, the two-lane road that would take me to Riverside Cemetery one hundred miles ahead.

I recalled the horrific winds the day of my father's burial. This time, no tumbleweeds confronted me; instead, a gentle tail-wind pushed me forward. Eventually I arrived at Enders, the tiny town in western Nebraska where Daddy and his family had attended church during the first five years of his life. In our last visit to the area, he had talked at length about the importance of those Sunday trips via the horse-drawn spring-wagon, trips of several miles cutting diagonally across the open prairie from their sod house homestead to church. He had shown me the farmhouse, still standing not far from town, where they often had been Sunday guests of another family for midday dinner after church. Connecting with neighbors on those Sundays must have been especially welcome for my grandmother after a long week of hard work caring for a family of six in the isolation of their prairie homestead.

The structure where Daddy and his family had attended church had been dismantled many years ago; the current Church of the Brethren congregation worshipped in a brick building, formerly the school, which had been updated for church use with a modern entry and a small addition. I parked alongside the grassy, fenced area Daddy had pointed out as the location of the original church. Over the years, trees had become established, providing welcome shade to this plot of greenery, now overgrown with wild grasses and weeds. Two weathered-grey, wooden outhouses remained, one in each of the two western corners of the lot. A house sparrow was perched in the ventilation opening high on the side of one outhouse.

Having taken in everything there, I climbed back into my car. It took only minutes to drive each of the hard-packed pea-gravel streets of town. Pioneer, Chase, and Lincoln streets ran north and south; streets running east and west were numbered. After I drove First, Second, Third, and Fourth streets, I had toured the town. In one yard tulips were blooming, not of the Emperor variety Daddy had planted and tended for decades, but tulips nonetheless. They welcomed me with their bright red hues. But the cemetery was not located here; I needed to drive on.

Along the way I noted the site of a long-gone building Daddy had told me a lot about. I immediately wished Daddy were with me to tell the stories again, for I could not recall the details. As I was berating myself, my negativity was interrupted by the joyful song of a meadowlark. The message was clear: focus on the positive energy of the moment. Once again, the world of nature provided a basic but profound lesson. My *search for the owl*, to gain wisdom about life, was resulting in numerous reminders of how to achieve a balanced, happy one. I recalled other lessons from recent months, including the benefits of delaying judgment and the ability to make great progress one small step at a time.

The road crossed the creek that would eventually meander past Riverside Cemetery. I was driving considerably below the speed limit, or I probably would not have seen it: something caught my eye in the water below. I parked the car some thirty feet from the bridge and slowly walked back to the two-lane, low-sided concrete structure, making as little sound as possible. There it was. A substantial beaver dam. Water tumbled musically over the spillway a third of the way out from the left bank. As it flowed toward the bridge, the waterway was ten feet wide. The calm pool created behind the dam was approximately thirty feet long: an oval shape with a tail where the creek entered upstream. Between me and the dam, a wire fence crossed the water, laced with last year's twining weeds. They hung decoratively and created ripples in the gentle flow of the waters emerging from the dam. Standing immobile and silent, I awaited my rewards. The first was a muskrat trailing his thin, furry tail. He glided effortlessly toward the bridge, dove mid-stream, disappearing out of sight. My eyes scanned the surface, awaiting his reappearance. I did not see him again. My attention was drawn to the mirror-surface oval. A pair of ducks emerged from the profusion of tall cattails and swam lazily across the pond. Beyond, the lush deep-green velvet of winter wheat formed a gentle backdrop for this idyllic scene. As I was ready to leave, a solitary red-winged blackbird lit on a prominent cattail growing close to the front of the dam and proceeded to serenade me. Had someone attempted to design the most aesthetically pleasing natural setting and to choreograph its living elements, it could not have been better. I was in awe of the quiet beauty of this place. How many local residents ever stopped to appreciate the treasure hidden in their midst?

Back in my car, I drove a couple of minutes, passing my maternal grandparents' farm before turning off the highway and heading north. I had chosen to drive the unpaved road along the Frenchman River; it was the longer, slower way to the cemetery, preferable for today's sentimental journey. I was in no hurry; in fact, I relished the opportunity to take my time. I had been concerned about mud on the dirt road, but there was no indication of recent rain. Dust prevailed. A small metal marker had been posted recently indicating this was "Road 730A." Ah, progress. To me, and to most who traveled it, this was simply *the river road*.

In May a few years ago, Daddy and I had seen our first-of-that-trip red-headed woodpecker pecking away at the thick, creviced bark of a mature cottonwood near the next bridge. The ancient trees growing along this portion of the Frenchman were a wonder to behold; on one trip Daddy and I had photographed their majestic forms. From the grassy road bank, a pink-eared cottontail eyed me as it lunched on tender blades of spring grass. Beyond the bridge lay the wide, familiar sweep of an alfalfa field, outlined by an arc of giant cottonwoods. These were owl trees if ever I had seen any. If this had been a movie, an owl would have appeared, gliding across the field toward me on its wide outstretched wings.

But it was not a movie; it was my real life. I drove slowly, my eyes searching the strong branches close to the tree trunks, but I spotted no owl. At the next bend in the road, I visually explored a small cornfield strewn with stalks from a prior year's crop. A few corncobs, neatly nibbled bare, lay there also. Mice. Owl food. But the owls, if they were there, stayed hidden, possibly watching me.

I was startled by a sudden flurry of wings. A flicker, not an owl, darted past the open window of my car, flashing its reddish-brown wing- and tail-feathers.

Several hundred yards beyond the cornfield, I saw yucca plants dotting the hillsides north of the road. Their tall spires were still upright, last year's dried seedpods intact. I parked. Stepping into the fine powder typical of this area's soil brought to mind the long, dusty walks along my grandfather's narrow farm lane, walks we city kids had taken to the mailbox to retrieve our grandparents' mail. Nowhere else on earth have I found soil to be so fine. I scrambled up the eroded bank to where the yuccas were growing. I was relieved to see plenty of the shiny black seeds. I gathered three seedpods; the brittle main stalk broke easily. I had a use for those seeds.

I returned to my car and drove on. As I progressed along the washboard surface, I drove with my right wheels in the powdery accumulation at its edge, thus avoiding some of the jarring of the endless parallel ruts. Proceeding at ten to fifteen miles per hour had two additional benefits: less dust was generated, and more sights could be observed.

The sun was attempting to appear, although so far it was merely a bright spot in the canopy of grey. The weather was cool but pleasant. Given the warmth of my car, I had long ago shed my coat.

As I traversed the five miles of river road, its familiar twists and turns, changing terrain, and crude bridges were old friends. As young children, my siblings and I had named each of the seven spans. One was the Potato Bridge, earned because driving across it had sounded to us like someone dumping out a bag of potatoes. These bridges were narrow and they lacked sides. Heavy wooden planks formed the bed across which one drove. The simplicity of their construction appealed to me.

Twenty-some years ago, my father had written an essay about his drive along this river road. He had brought a historical perspective to his writing that I lack. After his eighteen years living near here, he continued to visit this place, accruing many decades of memories. His roots were here; therefore, my roots are here, also. He and Mother had met in high school when her family moved to the area from Kansas. They had become high school sweethearts, then husband and wife, forming a marriage lasting sixty-seven years. Deep roots. No wonder I was drawn to this place today.

Further along the road and to the north rose rolling hills, capped with layers of undercut limestone shelves. A favorite family photograph shows Lois and me and our grandpa's farm dog Spotsie sitting atop one of those eroded rock ledges.

Wherever the winding road crossed the stream, trees clustered nearby. I spied a tidy nest in a crotch of bare branches. Elsewhere, another cottonwood with multiple trunks showed off its deeply furrowed bark. Its lower circumference was easily thirty feet. I could only guess at the age of the tree; it may have predated the first settlers in the area.

Ahead was a climb to a hilltop portion of the road. I downshifted as I started up the steep incline. One time we kids talked Daddy into putting our 1938 Plymouth into neutral and speeding down that hill. The rapidly accelerating ride was one of my earliest truly exhilarating experiences. I drove past the community's barren golf course with its sand greens, past some cattle, past more yuccas, across another bridge, and after a sharp hairpin turn to the right, I proceeded up the gentle rise and onto the paved road to Riverside Cemetery.

Its white perimeter fence looked neat and tidy. The native rock entry arch had been recently repaired and appeared stately and grand. My grandfather Mohler had helped to construct it as part of a Works Progress Administration project. I drove ceremoniously under the arch and down the gravel path lined on either side by ponderosa pines. Even though I had never lived in the region, I was familiar with the majority of surnames on the grave markers. I had heard my parents, as well as my grandparents, talk about those now memorialized by the stones.

I drove to the newer section of the cemetery and parked at the edge of the road close to Mom and Dad's side-by-side graves. In this non-irrigated, dry-land cemetery, native grasses required several years to reclaim a bare gravesite. Mom's, after three and a half years, had sparse vegetation. Daddy's site was barren, the powdery earth waiting for something to grow there.

I had brought flowers for their gravesites. Or more precisely, I had brought the *potential* for flowers. I had brought seeds…those of western wildflowers, plus the seeds I had harvested from the yuccas. I scattered them lovingly. I felt no need to control the end result. Over the past months, I had observed the rhythm and flow of the natural cycles of life, nature's inherent continuity. My roots were in this place; the physical remains of my mother and father were interred in its earth. Whether or not any of the seeds I had sown would germinate or the resulting plants survive mattered little. It was the gesture that mattered to me—in tune with nature's ways. I had made incredible progress in letting go of my need for control.

It was a beautiful, calm day. I sat on the prairie earth near their gravesites. Beyond the perimeter fence of the cemetery grew a new crop of winter wheat. Birds sang, taking pleasure in the shelter of the many trees. I heard the call of a mourning dove, but its brevity was akin to the shallowness of my sadness. The joyful lark song and delightful discoveries of the day had greater power and clearer messages for me. As I sat there, I marveled at my journey…yes, today's long drive, but more so the emotional journey of the past year. I was thankful I had chosen to experience the end of this year by visiting the cemetery. But mostly I was surprised to discover how little there was for me where Mother and Daddy were buried. I had felt their presence more keenly along the river road, while observing the quiet cottontail, and among the stout spires of yuccas. I had remembered them in the twists and turns of the road, in the stories associated with the rock ledges and the bridges. I was aware of the depth and breadth of the many memories of them I had experienced in the past several months. Although I was certain I would return to the cemetery, it would be more out of honor than out of my own need. My parents simply were not there.

I visited the gravesites of my maternal and paternal grandparents and those of the many aunts, uncles, and other relatives who were buried at the cemetery, including that of my Aunt Dolores who had preceded my father in death by nine days and whose funeral I had attended two days before he died. I made the gravestone rubbings I had come prepared to create.

When I was satisfied with my time at the cemetery, I drove on to nearby Wauneta. It had been home to my father after the sod house and throughout his high school years, and to his parents until they died. Because I had spent many childhood vacations visiting my grandparents, I had my own memories of the small town and was curious to explore it again.

The economy of many areas in rural America has suffered over the past decades. Such had been the case there as well. I parked near the north end of Tecumseh Avenue, the town's main street, and poked my head into the Wauneta Breeze office, home to the weekly newspaper. I walked south along the sidewalk, crossing at the corner with the only traffic light in town. As a child, my dad had made imprints of maple leaves in wet cement in front of the original telephone office. They were gone, victims of the heaving sidewalk, cracks, and numerous repairs. Chinese elm trees that were prevalent when I was young had died from Dutch elm disease years ago. Many of the buildings important to me no longer existed, including the house my grandfather built after Daddy's family moved into town. Even the river had been rechanneled in an effort at flood prevention, and Wauneta Falls itself was long gone. The people I had known there had either died or moved away. What I valued were the memories, the sense of history, and the sentiment I connected with the place. I found many of the changes disconcerting. Perhaps it is true: you cannot go back. Therefore, it was no surprise to me that it was not long before I was ready to move on.

I decided to drive back toward the cemetery along the river road before heading for home. I drove slowly, taking the opportunity to review the day. I had come a long way in my grief process, for today's emotions were neither disturbing nor sad. As I neared the turnoff to the cemetery, my reflective mood was interrupted. Something appeared in the road ahead at the crest of a hill. It was neither another vehicle nor a boy riding a bicycle, but something unexpected: two high-spirited horses were galloping toward me. One was white; one brown. Wearing no bridles, they proceeded unencumbered, frolicking merrily, prancing, and leaving twin clouds of dust in their wake. My car stopped almost by itself. I watched in awe as the two free spirits approached me, tossing their heads as they communicated with one another. Before reaching my car, they veered off, galloped up a rise to my left toward a cornfield, and disappeared. I sat there in stunned silence. Were these the wild horses Aunt Dolores had talked about in her glimpse into the afterlife? Had I missed the angels?

After a couple of minutes, I drove on; since it was on my way, I had decided to make a second stop at the cemetery.

Why had I returned, considering the several-hour drive ahead of me? In the long shadows across my parents' gravesites, I could see some of the seeds I had sown. Others may have been consumed by the birds that made this oasis their home. The fact pleased me. Within a few minutes, I was ready to go.

I had dedicated the day to honoring my dad's memory on the anniversary of his death. My dad had become the precious memories I held close to my heart. Therefore, my father would always be with me. He is a part of the spirit with which I live my life. There is no separation in death. Because I am and do and feel, he *is*, also.

And what of the owl? I had spent an entire year *in search of the owl*. Yes, I had observed two great horned owls in their natural habitat. But the goal of the quest was to discover not an owl, but the owl's wisdom as it relates to life: not only *life* as the opposite of *death*, but life as we experience it every day. Throughout the journey, the lessons I encountered enabled me to arrive at clear answers and to gain invaluable insights. I had been witness to the wondrous drama of the changing seasons, the predictability as well as the dependability of the countless miraculous cycles comprising the grandeur that is life, and the unequivocal continuity of human life through generation upon ongoing generation. The concept "death cannot happen unless something has been alive" resonated within me in a new way.

One more vital truth had been revealed: it is only the individual life that ends. Neither the willow tree, nor the great horned owl, nor the dearest of human beings is able to avoid death. Yet the grand scheme of life continues.

The elusive *owl* for which I had searched had sought me, also. We had found each other. Now it had come to roost, nestling inside me, willing to share its wisdom and quiet strength. On occasion, it still took wing, and I temporarily lost its guidance. But it always returned, its knowingness keeping me on course.

After leaving the white-fenced cemetery, I drove the short distance to the main road and turned west. It was late in the day, the time Daddy had died one year ago. The two-lane road aimed me straight toward the setting sun, transformed into a red orb by an overlay of thin clouds, clouds that drew chalky streaks on the blue slate of the sky. The pavement shimmered silver-red in the distance, vanishing into the brilliance of the end of day. The sustainer of all life on this planet, our sun, was beckoning me onward and bidding me farewell, urging me forward and reminding me to let go. Poignantly, I was driving into the sunset. I witnessed the brilliant orb being consumed by thickening clouds. Then, for the briefest of moments through a slim opening above the horizon, a curve emerged: the lower lip of a red mouth smiled at me...silently, knowingly.

The twilight that followed was quiet and serene. Night began to surround me and to escort me home. I was pleasantly tired. It had been a long day. It had been a long year.

I was looking forward to the days ahead, fully aware of the gift that is life.

ACKNOWLEDGMENTS

I may be the author, but bringing *In Search of the Owl* to fruition is the result of the influence, encouragement, effort, and expertise of many. My parents instilled in me the love of nature that is central to this book. My father's remarkable essence and loving ways caused me to miss him deeply and left me with memorable, poignant stories.

My sister, Lois, my brother, Robert, and I shared the experience of the death of our father and the loss of a guiding and loving force in our lives.

I am indebted to many who contributed in ways they may not have understood. After reading the opening pages of an early draft of my book, Michael (Mike) Henry, co-founder of Denver's Lighthouse Writer's Workshop, offered honest feedback that resulted in a significant improvement in the way the reader is introduced to my father. Years before the manuscript was in finished form, Susan Trausch, author of *Groping Toward Whatever or How I Learned to Retire (sort of)*, reacted positively to my voice in this writing. Anita Mumm of Mumm's the Word Editorial Services believed in the importance of the message: exploring the reality of grief and preparing others for the death of a loved one. Professional artist and friend Anna Kaye validated my intention to create graphite-and-ink drawings for the book. Anne Randolph introduced me to the Denver Woman's Press Club and expressed continued interest in my writing. I am also grateful for the support of my fellow poets in the Poetry Society of Colorado, especially Sandi Rhynard. My longtime friend Regina Dodge has always seen the best in me and encouraged my writing and other creative pursuits. Author of

Growing Myself Up, she honored me with one of the first copies of her memoir. I plan to do the same.

For moving the manuscript forward with their expertise, guidance, and attention to detail, I thank editor Alexandra O'Connell (Your Resident Wordsmith LLC) and proofreader Jennifer Jas (Words with Jas LLC). Alexandra offered enthusiastic support, a wealth of knowledge, and appreciation and understanding of my story as well as my voice and writing style.

Veronica Yager of YellowStudios LLC was the magician who designed the layout of the book and skillfully integrated my owl drawing into her beautiful cover design. She also shepherded me through the final stages and provided connections that led to the reality of the end product.

My daughter, Mindy, son-in-law Adam, and my grandsons, Samuel and Ashton, are living reminders of the continuity of life and family. These three descendants of my father and of me are precious beings who inhabit my life and help to fill it with energy and meaning.

A special thank you is due to my new husband, Jim, reader of drafts and patient listener, who provided heartfelt support and unending encouragement.

Mother Earth and her offspring…animal, plant, land, water, air…were always there for me, offering their healing qualities in my time of grief.

I am supremely grateful to the great horned owl whose strength of spirit stayed with me, guiding me through the first year without my dad.

And finally I wish to thank The Nature Conservancy and all of you who, by your beliefs and actions, serve as stewards of our planet earth and the vital balance of its ecosystem.

ABOUT THE AUTHOR

Jean E. Sidinger admits to having a lifelong love affair with words. She found it natural to keep an extensive handwritten journal following the death of her beloved father, a pioneer in the fields of wildlife management and ecology. She utilized the writing from that first year to create her thought-provoking memoir *In Search of the Owl*.

As a child, Jean learned to appreciate the world of the outdoors on Audubon field trips and during carefree days exploring her grandfather's Nebraska farm. Later in life, hiking and camping in the Rocky Mountains afforded time for writing and reflection. Throughout her life, she has shared her father's affinity for nature, so it is not surprising that she turned there for solace in her time of grief.

An educator by profession, Sidinger earned a PhD from the University of Denver. Her dissertation addressed audio-visual utilization by elementary classroom teachers. As a writer, she is known for her propensity to capture the tiniest nuances of her surroundings. Her poetry has appeared in *Quill and Parchment*, *Colorado Life* magazine, Poetry Society of Colorado's *Poets' Showcase: Winning Poems 2018–19*, and numerous anthologies. In 2011 as Artist in Residence at the Great Sand Dunes National Park and Preserve, her time was devoted to writing as well as creating two-dimensional art. An artist in the broadest sense, she is also a painter, jewelry maker, award-winning photographer, and former owner of Photographers' Gallery in Denver's Cherry Creek North. The graphite and ink illustrations for *In Search of the Owl* are hers.

She resides in Greenwood Village, Colorado, with her husband, Jim, also an accomplished photographer. *In Search of the Owl* is her first memoir.